# WT Poomsae
## World Class Poomsae Guide Book

예방의학사
YB HEALTH CARE & MEDICAL BOOKS

WTPTA
World Taekwondo Professional Trainer Association

# WT Poomsae
## World class Poomsae guide book

**초판 1쇄 인쇄** / 2022년 8월 1일
**초판 1쇄 발행** / 2022년 8월 1일

**저　자** : 임승민, 전민우, 강유진, 백형진, 김무성, 최나래, 이재희, 김혜준
**모　델** : 임승민, 전민우, 강유진, 최나래, 이재희, 김지수, 박지원, 박기현
**인쇄 · 편집** : 금강기획인쇄(02-2266-6750)

**문의처** : 010-4439-3169
**이메일** : prehabex@naver.com

**가　격**  20,000 원 / US $30 / CAD $35

※ 저자와의 협의에 의해 인지를 생략합니다.
※ 이 책은 저작권법에 의해 보호를 받는 저작물이므로 동영상 제작 및 무단전제와 복제를 금합니다.
※ 잘못된 책은 구입하신 서점에서 교환해 드립니다.

## 대표 저자.

### Rim, Seoungmin 임승민

- Head Coach, Canadian National Team
- Poomsae instructor, Pan American Taekwondo Union
- Former Ukraine National Team Coach
- Former instructor for the Ukraine defense ministry and ministry of internal affairs.
- Chartered Professional Coach of Canada
- Learning Facilitator, National Coaching Certification Program
- International Poomsae Referee
- 캐나다 국가대표 감독
- 팬암 태권도 연맹 품새 지도 위원
- 전) 우크라이나 국가대표 코치
- 전) 우크라이나 국방부, 내무부 지도사범
- 캐나다 공인 전문 스포츠 지도사
- 캐나다 국가 코치 자격 프로그램 지도 강사
- 품새 국제심판

### Jeon, Minwoo, Ph.D (전민우)

- President, WTPTA(World Taekwondo Professional Trainer Association)
- Korean National Team Coach
- Kyung-Hee University Poomsae Team Head Coach
- 현) WTPTA (세계태권도전문트레이너협회) 대표
- 2022 한국 대표팀 코치
- 현) 경희대학교 품새감독

### Kang Yujin (강유진)

- Head Master, Namchang Taekwondojang
- Triple crowned champion of the World Poomsae Championships, World University Games, World University Championships
- Ph.D candidate in Sports Science
- 현) 남창태권도장 수석사범
- 품새 국가대표 트리플 크라운 금메달리스트
- 서울대학교 사범대 스포츠과학전공 박사 수료

### Beak Hyoungjean (백형진)

- Adjunct professor, Dongguk University
- President, Preventive Exercise Association of Korea
- Ph.D, integrated medicine from Cha Medical University
- 동국대학교 산학협력 겸임교수
- 대한예방운동협회 협회장
- 차의과학대학교 통합의학 박사

### Kim Moosung (김무성)

- Secretary general, WTPTA
- General Manager, external affair, Seoul Bonbridge hospital
- Medial Vice Chair, Seoul Metropolitan City Taekwondo Association
- 현) WTPTA 사무국장
- 현) 서울본브릿지병원 대외협력 팀장
- 현) 서울특별시태권도협회 의무분과 부위원장

### Choi Narae (최나래)

- Director, WTPTA
- Head Master, Champion Taekwondojang
- Former WT Demonstration Team Member
- 현) WTPTA (세계태권도전문트레이너협회) 상무이사
- 현) 챔피언태권도장 수석사범
- 전) 세계태권도연맹시범단(WT) 단원
- 동덕여자대학교 체육학전공 석사 수료

### Lee Jaehee (이재희)

- Korean National Team Trainer, 2022 Asian Championships
- Korean National Team, 2015 Uiversiade
- Coach, KyungHee University Poomsae Team
- Korean National Team, 2014 Asian Taekwondo Poomsae Championships
- 2014 아시아태권도품새선수권대회 국가대표
- 2015 유니버시아드경기대회 태권도 품새국가대표
- 현) 경희대학교 품새부 코치
- 2022아시아태권도품새선수권 한국 대표팀 트레이너

### Kim Hyejun (김혜준)

- Director, WTPTA
- Former athletic trainer, Hanmam Plus Rehabilitation Clinic
- Former athletic trainer, Korea Racing Authority
- 현) WTPTA 상무이사
- 전) 한맘플러스 재활의학과의원 선수재활실 운동처방사
- 전) 한국마사회 기수협회 운동처방사

# Table of Contents
(목차)

Ⅰ. Introduction(서문) ································································· 05

Ⅱ. Ideal training structure for recognized Poomsae
   (공인품새에 적합한 컨디션 구성과정) ···························· 08
   1. Stretching & warm-up routine (스트레칭 및 웜업 루틴) ············ 09
   2. Poomsae specific functional exercises
      (공인품새를 위한 보강 운동) ·············································· 24
   3. Cool-down & static stretching (마무리 정적 스트레칭) ············ 43

Ⅲ. Poomsae(공인품새)
   1. Taegeuk 1 Jang(태극 1장) ················································ 46
   2. Taegeuk 2 Jang(태극 2장) ················································ 51
   3. Taegeuk 3 Jang(태극 3장) ················································ 57
   4. Taegeuk 4 Jang(태극 4장) ················································ 64
   5. Taegeuk 5 Jang(태극 5장) ················································ 70
   6. Taegeuk 6 Jang(태극 6장) ················································ 77
   7. Taegeuk 7 Jang(태극 7장) ················································ 84
   8. Taegeuk 8 Jang(태극 8장) ················································ 91
   9. Koryo(고려) ······································································ 99
   10. Keumgang(금강) ···························································· 109
   11. Taebaek(태백) ································································ 116
   12. Pyeongwon (평원) ·························································· 125
   13. Sipjin(십진) ···································································· 132
   14. Jitae(지태) ······································································ 141
   15. Chonkwon(천권) ···························································· 149
   16. Hansu(한수) ···································································· 159
   17. Ilyeo(일여) ······································································ 166

# Introduction
## 서문

After the 1st World Taekwondo Poomsae Championships held in Seoul, Korea, Taekwondo Poomsae has experienced an exponential growth in popularity and scale. It has been included in all the continental tournaments and has also been prominently featured in multi-sports events such as the Asian Games, Pan Am Games and Universiade's. It has been evident that Poomsae is included in most major Taekwondo events barring the Olympic Games.

However, the ambiguity of competition rules and systems lag behind the popularity and development of Poomsae competition on the global scale. In addition, the lack of scientific and developmentally appropriate training methods commonly leads to injuries of for Poomsae athletes with harmful consequences for their well-being.

This Poomsae training textbook by the World Taekwondo Professional Trainer Association functions as an informative resource for Poomsae coaches of all levels. Focusing on evidence-based training methods, this textbook aims to prevent training and competition-induced injuries and improve performance at the local, national, and international level.

Using English terminology, expressions, and commonly used phrases in English speaking dojangs, we strive to create an approachable resource for Taekwondo athletes of all levels.

I would like to thank the co-authors of this textbook along with the president of WTPTA, Dr. Minwoo Jeon. I would also like to express my sincere gratitude to all Taekwondo coaches from all corners of the world who equally share an unwavering love and passion for Taekwondo. I hope that this textbook can be an instrument to facilitate a better understand of competitive Poomsae and to Improve Poomsae coaching and training.

Lead author, **Seoung min Rim**

태권도 품새는 2006년 서울에서 열린 제1회 세계품새선수권대회 이후 양적으로나 질적으로 눈부시게 성장했습니다. 대륙별 대회는 물론이고 유니버시아드, 아시안 게임, 팬암 게임 등 종합 스포츠 경기에도 정식 종목으로 채택됨으로써 이제 올림픽을 제외한 모든 경기에 품새가 포함되어 있다고 할 수 있을 정도로 저변을 넓혀 왔습니다.

하지만 여전히 체계화되지 못한 모호한 경기 규정은 품새 수련 인구의 양적인 성장을 따라가지 못하고 있습니다. 수련 연령대 및 성장 단계에 따른 과학적 훈련 방법과 명확한 지침의 부재는 선수 부상의 단초를 제공할 뿐 아니라 수련자의 기저 건강에도 부정적인 영향을 끼칠 수 있습니다.

세계태권도전문트레이너협회에서 제작한 공인 품새 교본은 부상 예방과 경기력 향상을 위해 과학적으로 검증된 다양한 훈련 및 지도법을 품새 지도자 및 선수들에게 전달하고자 노력하였습니다.

비록 아직 태권도 품새 동작 용어가 영어로는 정리되지 않았지만 해외 수련생과 지도자들을 위해 실재 품새동작들을 최대한 이해하기 쉽도록 최대한 현장 용어를 사용하여 풀어 설명하였습니다.

본 교본이 출판되기까지 물심양면으로 노력한 전민우 대표 이하 공동 집필진에게 감사드리고, 더불어 태권도 보급과 발전을 위해 세계 각국에서 노력하고 계신 태권도인들에게 감사의 말씀을 전합니다. 본 교본을 통해 태권도 품새를 보다 명확하게 이해하고 품새 지도 및 수련에 많은 도움이 되길 기원합니다.

대표 저자 **임 승 민**

# WT Poomsae
World class Poomsae guide book

# II
## Ideal training structure for recognized Poomsae
### (공인품새에 적합한 컨디션 구성과정)

# Ideal training structure for recognized Poomsae
## 공인품새에 적합한 컨디션 구성 과정

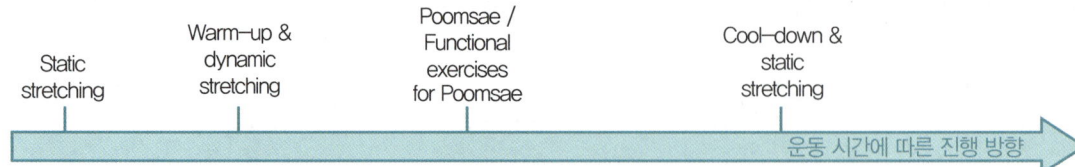

## 1. Stretching & warm-up routine (스트레칭 및 웜업 루틴)
1) Static stretching (정적 스트레칭)
2) Warm-up & dynamic stretching for Poomsae (공인품새를 위한 동적 스트레칭)

## 2. Poomsae specific functional exercises (공인품새를 위한 보강 운동)
1) Functional exercises of upper body (상체 보강 운동)
2) Functional exercises of core (코어 보강 운동)
3) Functional exercises of lower body (하체 보강 운동)
4) Functional exercises of balance (밸런스 보강 운동)

## 3. Cool-down & static stretching (마무리 정적 스트레칭)
Recognized Poomsae requires large range of motions. However, since it is difficult to achieve a sufficient range of motion with dynamic stretching, many Poomsae athletes perform static stretching before their competitions. Many studies have shown that static stretching may increase the risk of injuries as body temperature cools down. Static stretching just before the competition also reduces functionalities of movements. Therefore, it is recommended to perform dynamic stretching prior to daily training or competition followed by static stretching. It will increase the range of motion while providing muscle elasticity prior to the competition which will result in better performance during the competition.

The following chapters suggest static and dynamic stretching exercises and strength and conditioning program that will help to improve Poomsae athletes performance based upon understanding of movement mechanics and the functional anatomy of Poomsae athletes.

품새는 큰 관절가동범위가 필요한 종목 중 하나이다. 일반적으로 스트레칭의 목적과 그에 따른 종류, 효과 및 위험인자가 전혀 고려되지 않은 채 단순히 '근육을 늘려준다' 라는 개념에 의해서만 행해지고 있는 경우가 많다. 이처럼 목적 없는 스트레칭은 오히려 경기력과 근육 컨디션에 악영향의 요소로 작용될 수 있다.

경기 직전, 준비운동으로 정적 스트레칭만을 진행했을 때, 근육 유연성은 향상시키지만 근육과 관절의 지지력을 떨어뜨려 오히려 순간적인 힘을 내는 능력과 일반적인 근력 모두 감소시킬 수 있다. 또한, 정적 스트레칭만을 90초 이상 지속할 경우 상대적으로 근력 저하가 더 나타난다는 연구결과도 있다.

그렇다면 경기, 본 운동 직전에 적합한 컨디션 구성은 어떻게 진행되어야할까?

충분히 웜업(warm-up)되지 않은 근육과 신체 조직에 스트레칭을 하게 되면 최대 효과를 얻지 못하기 때문에 먼저 가볍게 웜업된 상태를 만든다. 핫팩, 고정식 자전거, 가벼운 조깅 등 다양한 방법 중, 상황에 맞게 선택하여 근육의 온도를 높인다.

그 다음 단계로, 정적 스트레칭(static stretching)과 동적 스트레칭(dynamic stretching)을 적용하여 웜업과 스트레칭이 함께 이루어지도록 한다.

동적 스트레칭은 품새에 필요한 관절가동범위를 만들어내며, 시합 전 적절한 근육의 탄성을 주어 근육의 활성도를 향상시키고, 기능적인 효율성을 증진시켜 경기력 향상에 큰 도움이 될 것이다. 그러나 일반적인 동적 스트레칭 방법으로는 태권도, 특히 품새에서 필요한 관절가동범위를 만들어내기에는 어려움이 있다. 따라서 품새에 특화된 동적 스트레칭이 필요하다. 우리는 품새 선수의 기능적 특성을 의과학적으로 분석한 〈품새 선수를 위한 정적, 동적 스트레칭, 보강 운동〉을 제시하려고 한다.

# 1. Stretching & warm-up routine
## 스트레칭 및 웜업 루틴

### 1) Static stretching (정적 스트레칭)

Static stretching is a widely known technique that passively stretches the muscles for an extended period of time. The ideal time to maintain stretched position ranges from as little as 3 second to 60 seconds and the some studies have shown that the most effective duration for static stretching is between 15-30 seconds.

Static stretching is safer than other types of stretching as you can control the limit of elasticity of joints, tendons and ligaments. Static stretching is the recommended stretching method for beginner practitioners; however, excessive static stretching may induce inhibited stretch reflexes, slower reaction times, increased muscle-tendon compliance, and the decrease in strength. Furthermore, many recent studies on the topic have also revealed that static stretching before activity is not associated with significant injury reductions. Excessive static stretching prior to training or competition is not recommended.

For Poomsae athletes, iliopsoas, rectus femoris, lumbar quadriceps, erector spinae, gastrocnemius, and extensor digitorum longus are functionally important muscles and the following chapter introduces effective and safe static stretching exercises.

정적 스트레칭 기법은 매우 효과적이고, 보편적으로 사용되는 스트레칭 기법 중 하나이다. 이는 해당 근육을 수동적으로 최대 스트레칭하여 연장된 시간 동안 유지하는 방법이다. 스트레칭된 자세를 유지하는 최적 시간은 적게는 3초부터 많게는 60초로 알려져 있고, 근육의 유연성을 향상시키는 가장 효과적인 스트레칭 유지 시간은 15~30초라는 연구 결과가 있다.

정적 스트레칭은 다른 스트레칭 기법보다 스스로 통제할 수 있기 때문에 관절의 신장성 한계를 넘는 위험이 적다. 이러한 정적 스트레칭은 초심자에게 훌륭한 스트레칭 기법이지만, 과도한 정적 스트레칭은 오히려 신장 반사 수축을 일으키게 된다. 따라서 운동 전 과도한 정적 스트레칭은 피하는 것이 좋다.

임상에서의 품새 선수들이 가지고 있는 질환은 다른 종목에 비해 뚜렷하게 나타난다. 대부분의 품새 선수에게 엉덩허리근, 넙다리곧은근, 허리네모근, 척주세움근, 장딴지근, 긴엄지폄근 등 근육 과사용으로 인한 근육 단축 현상을 쉽게 볼 수 있다. 이 특성들을 중점적으로 하여 품새 선수에게 특히 필요한 정적 스트레칭으로 구성하였기에 현장에서 적극 활용하였으면 한다.

# 1. Stretching & warm-up routine
## 스트레칭 및 웜업 루틴

### (1) Standing extensor digitorum longus, tibialis anterior stretching

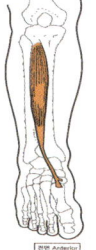 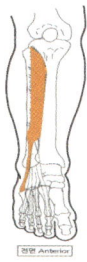   

① From walking stance, roll your foot so that the top of your foot touches the mats.
② Point your heel to the outside of your body (left or right side).
③ Repeat the motion by turning the foot in the 1st position.

① 서서 한쪽 발을 뒤로 뻗고, 발목관절을 발바닥굽힘 상태로 바닥에 밀착시킨다.
② 그 상태로 20초 동안 자세를 유지한 후, 반대쪽 방향을 실시한다.
③ 1번 자세에서 발을 안쪽번짐시켜 동작을 반복한다.

> Caution : Roll your toes and straighten your knees.
> 주의사항 : 발가락이 둥글게 만든다. 무릎관절을 편다.

### (2) Standing gastrocnemius, hamstring stretching

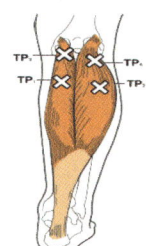   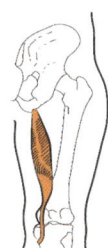 

① Starting in a position slightly shorter than walking stance, raise your toes off of the mat and reach down keeping your knees straight.
② Maintain a position where your hips are square to the floor.
③ After holding this posture for 20 seconds, perform with the other leg.

① 서서 한쪽 발을 앞으로 뻗고, 발목관절을 발등굽힘 상태로 만들어 손으로 고정한다.
② 골반의 앞쪽 기울임을 유지하며 몸통을 굽힌다.
③ 그 상태로 20초 동안 자세를 유지한 후, 반대쪽 방향을 실시한다.

> Caution : Straighten your knees. Keep your back straight.
> 주의사항 : 무릎관절을 편다. 허리를 둥글게 굽히지 않는다.

# 1. Stretching & warm-up routine
## 스트레칭 및 웜업 루틴

### (3) Pigeon pose hip rotator stretching

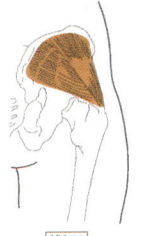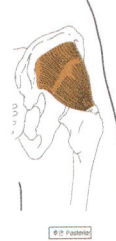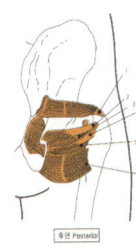

① From a seated position, bend your leading leg 90 degrees and externally rotate hip joint.
② Rotate your torso in the direction of your bent knee and lower your upper body.
③ After holding this posture for 20 seconds, perform with the other leg.

① 앉아서 한쪽 무릎관절을 90°로 굽힘하고, 엉덩관절을 가쪽돌림시켜 준비자세를 만든다.
② 구부린 무릎 방향으로 몸통을 회전시켜 골반을 밀어낸다.
③ 그 상태로 20초 동안 자세를 유지한 후, 반대쪽 방향을 실시한다.

> **Caution :** Push the pelvis in the direction of your calf and the floor. Do not bend your back excessively.
> 주의사항 : 골반을 반대 방향으로 밀어 넣어준다. 허리를 과하게 앞으로 숙이지 않도록 한다.

### (4) Half kneeling position psoas, quadriceps femoris stretching

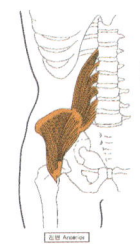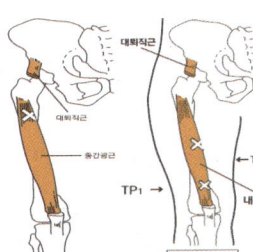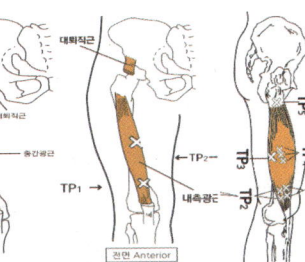

① Starting out in a position similar to long stance, drop your back knee onto the ground.
② Push your pelvis forward and hold for 20 seconds.
③ Grasp your back leg close to your ankle and continue pushing your hips forward.
④ After holding this posture for another 20 seconds, repeat with the other leg.

① 한쪽 무릎을 꿇은 상태에서 반대쪽의 무릎을 지면에 밀착시킨다.
② 앞에 세운 무릎을 앞으로 구부리며, 골반을 앞으로 밀어낸다.
③ 자세를 고정한 후, 손으로 뒤쪽 다리의 발목을 잡아당겨 무릎을 구부린다.
④ 그 상태로 20초 동안 자세를 유지한 후, 반대쪽 방향을 실시한다.

> **Caution :** Keep your pelvis straight and fixed so your back is kept straight. Ensure that your front leg does not tilt towards the inside of your body.
> 주의사항 : 골반이 좌, 우로 틀어지지 않도록 유지한다. 허리를 앞으로 숙이지 않도록 고정한다.
> 앞에 세운 다리가 과하게 안으로 들어가지 않도록 한다.

# 1. Stretching & warm-up routine
## 스트레칭 및 웜업 루틴

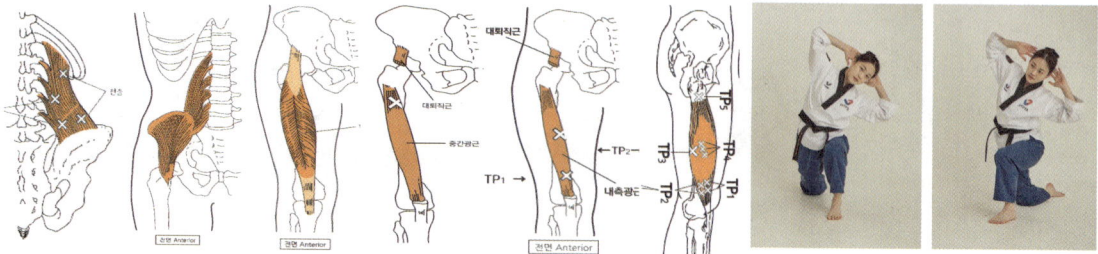

### (5) Half kneeling position quadratus lumborum, psoas, quadriceps femoris stretching

① Kneel with one knee on the mats.
② Bend your front knee and push your pelvis forward.
③ Fix your arms behind your head, tilt your upper body to the side and hold the posture for 20 seconds, then perform with the opposite leg.

① 한쪽 무릎을 꿇은 상태에서 반대쪽의 무릎을 지면에 밀착시킨다.
② 앞에 세운 무릎을 앞으로 구부리며, 골반을 앞으로 밀어낸다.
③ 팔을 머리 뒤에 고정한 상태로, 상체를 옆으로 기울여 20초 동안 자세를 유지한 후,
   다시 돌아와 반대쪽 방향을 실시한다.

> Caution : Keep your pelvis straight. Position your waist so that it does not bend forward and tilt your upper body to the side.
> 주의사항 : 골반이 좌, 우로 틀어지지 않도록 유지한다. 허리를 앞으로 숙이지 않도록 고정하며 상체를 옆으로 기울인다.

### (6) Standing hamstring stretching (2 motions)

  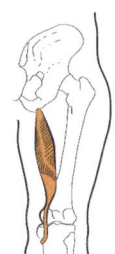   

① While standing, stretch one foot forward, straighten your knee, and fix your foot in dorsiflexion.
② Maintain an anterior tilt of the pelvis, bend your waist and hold the posture for 20 seconds, then perform with the opposite leg.
③ Return to the step 1 position and repeat step 2 position by rotating upper body toward the lifted leg.
④ After holding this posture for another 20 seconds, repeat with the other leg.

① 서서 한쪽 발을 앞으로 뻗어 무릎관절을 펴고, 발목관절을 발등굽힘시켜 고정한다.
② 골반의 앞쪽 기울임을 유지하여 몸통을 굽힘하여 20초 동안 자세를 유지한다.
③ 1번 자세로 다시 돌아온 다음, 올린 다리 쪽의 방향으로 몸통을 회전하며 2번 자세를 반복한다.
④ 그 상태로 20초 동안 자세를 유지한 후, 반대쪽 방향을 실시한다.

> Caution : Keep your back straight. Maintain an anterior tilt of the pelvis.
> 주의사항 : 허리를 둥글게 말며 굽힘하지 않는다. 골반의 앞쪽 기울임을 유지한다.

# 1. Stretching & warm-up routine
## 스트레칭 및 웜업 루틴

### (7) Seated hamstring, adductor, quadratus lumborum stretching

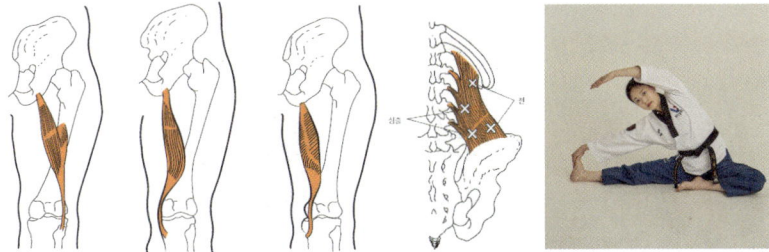

① With one knee bent, straighten the other knee. Fix your feet in dorsiflexion.
② Bend your back and hold the posture for 20 seconds. Repeat with the other leg.
③ Repeat the motion by tilting your upper body sideways in the first position.

① 한쪽 무릎관절을 굽힘한 상태에서 반대쪽 무릎관절을 펴고 앉아,
   발목관절을 발등굽힘 상태로 만들어 손으로 고정한다.
② 손을 머리 위에 뻗어 고정한 후, 상체를 옆으로 기울인다.
③ 그 상태로 20초 동안 자세를 유지한 후, 반대쪽 방향을 실시한다.

> Caution : Make sure your hips stay in contact with the floor.
> When your upper body is tilted to the side, fix your upper body to face forward.
> 주의사항 : 골반이 바닥과 떨어지지 않도록 한다. 상체를 옆으로 기울인 자세에서는 상체가 앞을 보도록 고정한다.

### (8) Standing erector spinae, quadratus lumborum, latissimus dorsi stretching

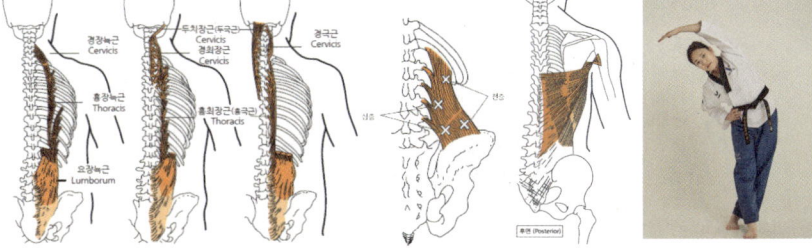

① While standing, put one leg to cross legs each other.
② Extend your arm upward and tilt your upper body to the side.
③ After holding the posture for 20 seconds in that position, perform in the opposite direction.

① 서서 한쪽 다리를 뒤로 꼬아 고정한다.
② 손을 머리 위에 뻗어 고정한 후, 상체를 옆으로 기울인다.
③ 그 상태로 20초 동안 자세를 유지한 후, 반대쪽 방향을 실시한다.

> Caution : Keep your legs parallel and shift your weight with your pelvis.
> 주의사항 : 두 다리가 11자가 되도록 한다. 골반과 함께 중심 이동을 해야 한다.

# 1. Stretching & warm-up routine
## 스트레칭 및 웜업 루틴

### (9) Standing upper trapezius, sternocleidomastoid stretching (2 motions)

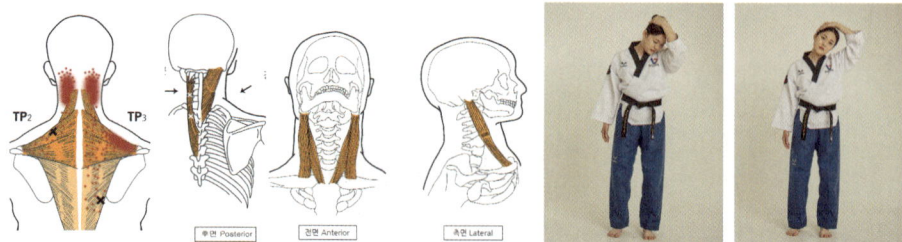

① Reach above your head with your right hand and hold the left side of your head. Bring your head to the right side slowly.
② Hold this position for 20 seconds with no excessive force.
③ Repeat for the other side of the neck.

① 서서 한쪽 손으로 머리를 잡고, 45°로 목을 돌려 시선을 내려본 준비자세를 만든다.
② 그 상태로 20초 동안 자세를 유지한 후, 반대쪽 방향을 실시한다.
③ 정면을 본 상태로 동작을 반복한다.

> Caution : Make sure to keep your opposite shoulder down. Do not use excessive force to stretch the neck.
> 주의사항 : 반대 쪽 어깨가 함께 올라가지 않도록 하강하여 고정한다. 목을 과하게 힘줘서 굽힘하지 않는다.

### (10) Standing pectoralis major & minor stretching (2 motions)

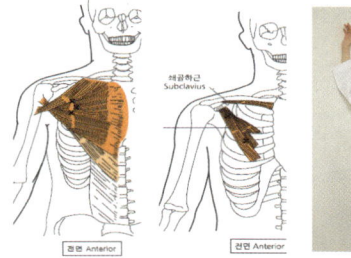

① Stand and raise one arm and place it on the wall, making a 90 degree angle with your elbow.
② Rotate your whole torso in the opposite direction and maintain this posture for 20 seconds, then perform the opposite direction.
③ Repeat the motion by placing your arm higher on the wall.

① 서서 한쪽 팔을 들어 어깨관절 90° 벌림, 팔꿈관절 90° 굽힘하여 벽에 고정한다.
② 한쪽 무릎관절을 굽힘하며, 몸통 전체를 반대로 회전해 20초 동안 자세를 유지한 후, 반대쪽 방향을 실시한다.
③ 어깨관절 120° 벌림, 팔꿈관절 120° 굽힘하여 벽에 고정해 동작을 반복한다.

> Caution : Make sure that the arm does not start behind your torso.
> Keep your pelvis straight.
> 주의사항 : 팔만 뒤로 빠지는 동작이 되지 않도록 한다. 허리를 앞으로 숙이면서 골반을 뒤로 빼지 않도록 한다.

# 1. Stretching & warm-up routine
## 스트레칭 및 웜업 루틴

### 2) Warm-up & dynamic stretching for recognized Poomsae
   (공인품새를 위한 동적 스트레칭)

Dynamic stretching is a technique that uses well-controlled elastic movements to move body parts up to the limit of the limits of the ranges of motion.

Dynamic stretching involves eccentric movements with gradual increases of rages of motion.

It is not uncommon to see Poomae athletes, particularly amongst recognized Poomsae athletes, perform static stretching exercises before competition to increase their range of motion. As previously explained, from functional standpoint, static stretching may be ineffective. Moreover, it may increase the risk of injuries.

We have researched and experimented stretching exercises that are effective in increasing range of motion while being highly functional for Poomsae athletes. These individualized Poomsae-specific warm-up and dynamic stretching exercises function to increase performance while reducing the risk of injuries.

동적 스트레칭은 운동 범위의 제한 지점까지 신체 부분을 움직이기 위하여 잘 조절된 탄성 운동을 이용하는 스트레칭 기법 중 하나이다.

이는 목적성이 있는 신장성 동작이다. 즉, 탄력 있는 동작이 점진적으로 증진되어야 하지만, 무분별한 과도한 증진이 아닌 조절된 움직임에 의한 증진이여야 한다는 것이다.

현장에서 많은 품새 선수들이 관절가동범위를 위하여 정적 스트레칭 위주로 몸을 풀고 바로 본 운동 혹은 경기에 임한다. 앞서 말했듯, 경기 직전의 정적 스트레칭만으로 구성된 준비 운동은 오히려 운동의 기능적 효율을 떨어지게 할 가능성이 높다. 즉, 근육이 오히려 쿨 다운(cool-down)되어 부상 확률이 높아질 수 있다는 말이기도 하다.

우리는 경기 직전 품새에 필요한 충분한 관절가동범위가 나오게 함과 동시에 근육에 적절한 탄성을 주어 기능적 효율성을 증진시킬 수 있는 '품새 선수를 위한 동적 스트레칭'을 연구하였다. 이는 종목의 특성에 따라 차별화를 둔 웜업(warm-up)과 동적 스트레칭이기에 기능적 효율 증진과 함께 경기력 향상, 부상 예방에 도움이 될 것이다.

# 1. Stretching & warm-up routine
## 스트레칭 및 웜업 루틴

### (1) 3 Step hip circumduction - small arc (2 motions)

① Take 3 steps after each repetition of this exercise.
② Lift your rear leg and make a circle by bringing your knee across your body and to the outside, and finishing by dropping your leg beside you drop your leg beside you.
③ Take 3 steps forward, and repeat with your other leg.
④ Lift your rear leg and make a circle in other direction.

① 3 스텝 밟으면서 앞으로 전진하며 동작을 실시한다.
② 한 쪽 무릎관절을 굽힘한 채로 다리를 바깥쪽으로 크게 돌려준다.
③ 3 스텝 밟으며 전진 후, 반대쪽도 동일하게 수행한다.
④ 동일한 방법으로 다리를 안쪽으로 돌려주며 반복하여 진행한다.

> Caution : Proceed until hip joint feels more limber.
> Benefits : Improvement of hip joint mobility while warming up the body.
> 주의사항 : 관절을 크게 돌려준다는 느낌으로 진행한다.
> 효과 : 엉덩관절 가동성 증진 및 웜업.

### (2) 3 Step hip circumduction - big arc (2 motions)

① Take 3 steps after each repetition of this exercise.
② While keeping your standing leg straight, externally rotate your hip by drawing a big circle with your other leg.
③ Take 3 steps forward, and repeat with your opposite leg.
④ On the way back, perform the same steps with hip internal rotation.

① 3 스텝 밟으면서 앞으로 전진하며 동작을 실시한다.
② 한 쪽 무릎관절을 편 채로 다리를 바깥쪽으로 크게 돌려준다.
③ 3 스텝 밟으며 전진 후, 반대쪽도 동일하게 수행한다.
④ 동일한 방법으로 다리를 안쪽으로 돌려주며 반복하여 진행한다.

> Caution : Focus on maximizing the range of motion in your hips.
> Benefits : Improvement of hip joint mobility while warming up the body.
> 주의사항 : 관절을 크게 돌려준다는 느낌으로 진행한다.
> 효과 : 엉덩관절 가동성 증진 및 웜업.

# 1. Stretching & warm-up routine
## 스트레칭 및 웜업 루틴

### (3) 1 Step hip flexion in 3 directions (short motion)

① Take 1 step after each repetition of this exercise.
② Raise your leg forward while straightening your knees and alternate your legs.
③ Raise your leg sideways while straightening your knees and alternate your legs.
④ Raise your legs inwards across your body while straightening your knees and alternate your legs.

① 짧게 1 스텝 밟으면서 앞으로 전진하며 동작을 실시한다.
② 무릎관절을 편 채로 다리를 앞으로 짧게 번갈아 뻗어준다.
③ 동일한 방법으로 다리를 옆으로 짧게 번갈아 뻗어준다.
④ 동일한 방법으로 다리를 안으로 짧게 번갈아 뻗어준다.

Caution : Perform all movements with a fixed torso and pelvis so that they are facing forward.
Benefits : Improvement of hip joint mobility while warming up the body.
주의사항 : 몸통과 골반이 앞을 보도록 고정하여 모든 동작을 진행한다.
효과 : 엉덩관절 가동성 증진 및 웜업.

### (4) 1 Step hip flexion in 2 directions (long motion)

① Lift your leg up quickly.
② Rotate your leg outward to create a large range of motion.
③ Repeat the exercise and rotate your leg inward.

① 짧게 1 스텝 밟으면서 앞으로 전진하며 동작을 실시한다.
② 무릎관절을 편 채로 다리를 바깥쪽으로 크게 돌려주며 번갈아 길게 끌어 올려 찬다.
③ 동일한 방법으로 다리를 안쪽으로 크게 돌려주며 번갈아 길게 끌어 올려 찬다.

Caution : Lift your leg up high and maximize range of motion.
Benefits : Improvement of hip joint mobility while warming up the body.
주의사항 : 끌어올려 길게 차도록 한다.
효과 : 엉덩관절 가동성 증진 및 웜업.

# 1. Stretching & warm-up routine
## 스트레칭 및 웜업 루틴

### (5) Cross walking & trunk rotation

① From a position similar to walking stance, reach down toward your toes.
② Raise the arm opposite to your front leg toward the ceiling while trying to keep your hips square to the ground. Raise and lower your arm 3 times.
③ Rotate your torso toward the direction of the leading foot.
④ Stand up and step forward to repeat the exercise on your opposite side.

① 팔꿈관절을 서로 잡아 상체를 고정시키고, 다리를 꼬아 상체를 숙인다.
② 고정한 팔을 바닥 쪽으로 3번 반동을 준다.
③ 앞쪽 발의 방향으로 몸통을 회전시켜준다.
④ 그대로 일어나 앞으로 나아가며 반대 다리를 꼬아 반복한다.

> Caution : Do not apply excessive force while performing the movement.
> Benefits : Stretches the knee and gastrocnemius muscles,
>                improves trunk mobility while warming up the body.
> 주의사항 : 무리한 강도로 반동을 주지 않는다.
> 효과 : 뒤넙다리근, 장딴지근 스트레칭, 몸통 가동성 증진 및 웜업.

### (6) Front lunge & chest to foot

① From a position similar to long stance, drop your back knee onto the ground.
② While trying to keep your pelvis in a stationary position, push your hips as far forward as possible.
③ Next, move your hips back while straightening your front knee.
④ Return your body to the first position and repeat with your opposite leg.

① 동적 프론트 런지를 1번 한다.
② 런지의 앉는 동작으로 이어져서, 뒤의 무릎을 바닥에 고정하고
    앞의 무릎을 구부려 골반을 밀어 넣어준다.
③ 이어서 앞의 구부러진 무릎을 펴서 뒤로 그대로 앉아 몸통을 구부린다.
④ 그대로 일어나 나아가며 반대쪽도 동일하게 진행한다.

> Caution : Ensure dorsiflexion of the rear leg in step 3.
> Benefits : Improvement of hip joint and T-spine mobility while warming up the body.
> 주의사항 : 3번 자세에서 뒤에 위치한 발은 발바닥굽힘 상태로 진행한다.
> 효과 : 엉덩관절, 몸통 가동성 증진 및 웜업.

# 1. Stretching & warm-up routine
## 스트레칭 및 웜업 루틴

### (7) Side lunge & stand up

① Do a dynamic side lunge.
② Stand up and step forward with the leg that was bent and do another side lunge, bending your other leg.
③ Make sure you are stepping toward the same wall each time.

① 동적 사이드 런지를 한다.
② 그대로 밀어주는 힘으로 일어나면서 앞으로 회전하며 반대 발로 동적 사이드 런지를 한다.
③ 옆으로 나아가며 번갈아 진행한다.

> Caution : Do not turn your torso. Maintain tension in your core muscles.
> Benefits : Stretches knee muscle and adductor muscle, improves hip joint mobility while warming up the body.
> 주의사항 : 몸통이 돌아가지 않도록 수행한다. 코어근육에 긴장감을 유지한다.
> 효과 : 뒤넙다리근, 엉덩관절 모음근 스트레칭, 엉덩관절 가동성 증진, 웜업 및 근육 탄력성 증진.

### (8) Side kick & Side kick motion with hip push

① Get into the posture for a sidekick.
② Hold your knee and push your hips forward.
③ Alternate legs and move forward.

① 옆차기 준비자세를 만든다.
② 무릎을 고정하여 골반을 밀어 넣어준다.
③ 앞으로 전진하며 번갈아 진행한다.

> Caution : Gradually increase force to avoid injury.
> Benefits : Improvement of hip joint mobility while warming up the body.
> 주의사항 : 처음부터 과도하게 진행하지 않고, 점진적으로 진행한다.
> 효과 : 엉덩관절 가동성 증진 및 웜업.

# 1. Stretching & warm-up routine
## 스트레칭 및 웜업 루틴

### (9) Kick & T-balance

① From kicking stance, perform a stretch kick to the front.
② Without touching the floor, bring your leg down and swing it back. Make a T-shape by lowering your upper body.
③ Return to kicking stance and do the same motions for your opposite side.

① 한 쪽 발을 길게 끌어올려 찬다.
② 다리는 바닥에 닿지 않고 그대로 내려와 뒤로 뻗으며, 상체를 숙여 T자 모양을 만든다.
③ 다리를 다시 내려 반대쪽도 동일하게 진행한다.

Caution : Make sure that your torso and pelvis are square with the floor and do not rotate.
Benefits : Stretches hamstrings, improves hip joint mobility while warming up the body.
주의사항 : 몸통과 골반이 열리며 돌아가지 않도록 진행한다.
효과 : 뒤넙다리근 스트레칭, 엉덩관절 가동성 증진 및 웜업.

### (10) Hip internal rotation in frog position

① Make a frog position with your knees spread apart and bent at 90 degrees.
② Move your pelvis back and forth repeatedly.
③ Rotate your hip joints one at a time by lifting your foot to the ceiling.
④ Repeat as needed.

① 바닥에 엎드려 개구리자세를 만든다.
② 앞. 뒤로 골반을 움직여준다.
③ 엉덩관절을 한 쪽씩 안쪽돌림한다.
④ 이를 반복하여 진행한다.

Caution : Fix your torso and pelvis so that they do not twist.
Benefits : Improves the mobility of your pelvis and hip joints while warming up the body.
주의사항 : 몸통과 골반을 틀어지지 않게 고정하여 진행한다.
효과 : 골반, 엉덩관절 가동성 증진 및 웜업.

## 1. Stretching & warm-up routine
### 스트레칭 및 웜업 루틴

### (11) Hip external rotation with hamstrings stretching and hip mobility exercise

① Sit with one knee bent and with your hip joint rotated externally.
② Bend your torso toward the extended leg.
③ Return to the first position then bend your body forward without altering your posture.
④ Bring your body back up, lift your hips off the ground, and push your pelvis forward
⑤ Repeat this exercise and do the same for the other side.

① 한쪽 무릎관절을 굽힘하고, 엉덩관절을 가쪽돌림한 상태로 앉는다.
② 반대 다리 쪽으로 몸통을 그대로 굽힘하여 유지한 후에, 팔을 위로 뻗어 고정한 채로 몸통을 옆으로 기울인다.
③ 다시 제자리로 돌아와서 앞으로 몸통을 굽힘한다.
④ 다시 제자리로 돌아와서 골반을 넣어주며 일어난다.
⑤ 이를 반복하여 반대쪽도 동일하게 진행한다.

**Caution :** Focus on the movement of the hip joint.
**Benefits :** Stretches hamstrings, adductor and quadriceps. Maximizes mobility and warms up the hip joint.
주의사항 : 엉덩관절의 움직임에 집중하여 진행한다.
효과 : 뒤넙다리근, 엉덩관절 모음근, 허리네모근 스트레칭, 엉덩관절 가동성 최대 증진 및 웜업.

### (12) Hip internal rotation with hamstrings stretching and hip mobility exercise

① Sit with one knee bent and with your hip joint rotated inward.
② Bend your torso toward the extended leg.
③ Return to the first position then bend your body forward without altering your posture.
④ Bring your body back up, lift your hips off the ground, and push your pelvis forward.
⑤ Repeat this and do the same for the other side.

① 한쪽 무릎관절을 굽힘하고, 엉덩관절을 안쪽돌림한 상태로 앉는다.
② 반대 다리 쪽으로 몸통을 그대로 굽힘하여 유지한 후에, 팔을 위로 뻗어 고정한 채로 몸통을 옆으로 기울인다.
③ 다시 제자리로 돌아와서 앞으로 몸통을 굽힘한다.
④ 다시 제자리로 돌아와서 골반을 넣어주며 일어난다.
⑤ 이를 반복하여 반대쪽도 동일하게 진행한다.

**Caution :** Focus on the movement of the hip joint.
**Benefits :** Stretches hamstrings, adductor and quadriceps. Maximizes mobility and warms up the hip joint.
주의사항 : 엉덩관절의 움직임에 집중하여 진행한다.
효과 : 뒤넙다리근, 엉덩관절 모음근, 허리네모근 스트레칭, 엉덩관절 가동성 최대 증진 및 웜업.

# 1. Stretching & warm-up routine
## 스트레칭 및 웜업 루틴

### (13) Hip mobility in frog position with one leg straight

① Make a frog pose with one leg straight.
② Move your pelvis back and forth repeatedly.
③ Repeat the exercise with your alternate leg straight.

① 바닥에 엎드려, 한 쪽 다리를 편 개구리자세를 만든다.
② 앞, 뒤로 골반을 움직여준다.
③ 반대쪽도 동일하게 진행한다.

> Caution : Fix your torso and pelvis so that they do not twist.
> Benefits : Improves mobility of your pelvis and hip joints while warming up your body.
> 주의사항 : 몸통과 골반을 틀어지지 않게 고정하여 진행한다.
> 효과 : 골반, 엉덩관절 가동성 최대 증진 및 웜업.

### (14) Seated split stretching & mobility

① Sit with your legs wide apart in a straddle position.
② Tilt your pelvis back and forth.
③ Rotate your body to the left and right into front splits.
③ Repeat this process.

① 다리를 본인 기준 최대로 벌리고 앉는다.
② 그 상태에서 골반을 앞, 뒤로 움직여준다.
③ 이어서 왼쪽, 오른쪽으로 몸통을 회전시켜 골반도 밀어 넣어준다.
④ 이를 반복하여 진행한다.

> Caution : Focus on the movement of the pelvis and hip joints.
> Benefits : Improves mobility of your pelvis and hip joints while warming up your body.
> 주의사항 : 골반과 엉덩관절의 움직임에 집중하여 진행한다.
> 효과 : 골반, 엉덩관절 가동성 최대 증진 및 웜업.

# 1. Stretching & warm-up routine
## 스트레칭 및 웜업 루틴

### (15) Side split stretching & mobility

① Get into a straddle position.
② Move your pelvis back and forth.
③ Repeat this process.

① 다리를 본인 기준 최대로 벌리고 앉는다.
② 그 상태에서 골반을 앞, 뒤로 밀어 넣으며 움직여준다.
③ 이를 반복하여 진행한다.

Caution : Focus on the movement of the pelvis and hip joints.
Benefits : Improves mobility of your pelvis and hip joints while warming up your body.
주의사항 : 골반과 엉덩관절의 움직임에 집중하여 진행한다.
효과 : 골반, 엉덩관절 가동성 최대 증진 및 웜업.

## 2. Poomsae specific functional exercises
### 공인품새를 위한 보강 운동

It is ineffective to provide non-specific strength and conditioning programs without considering distinctive differences in functionality of each sport. The following exercises are specifically designed for recognized Poomsae athletes.

### The need for joint stability training and strength training for recognized Poomsae athletes

Functional stability refers to the ability to maintain alignment of the body when there is an external force or change. This ability is essential for improving the performance of the Poomsae player because it keeps one part of the body stable while extending and contracting an adjacent part of the body, enabling consistent posture and speed.

To improve functional stability, an athlete requires balance, strength and endurance. These requirements are also an important factor in developing and maintaining consistently strong performance.

Along with good mobility, strengthening joint muscles and increasing stability allows Poomsae athletes to establish the foundation for efficient power and elastic energy in the muscles, leading to stronger and more accurate Poomsae movements.

### The need for balance training for recognized Poomsae athletes

The human body's balance system mainly consists of ocular-motor, vestibular, and somatosensory systems of the nervous system. Compared to the ocular-motor and vestibular systems, the somatosensory systems (including proprioceptive sensory) are lesser known balance system for practitioners. To explain this easily, the proprioceptive sense refers to conscious and unconscious recognition of the position of a joint, acting as a sensor in the muscles, tendons, and ligaments. It reacts instantly to movement and sends signals to the central nervous system, resulting in rapid motor responses to the initial movement stimulus. Therefore, the proprioceptive sense is essential for balance training and improving the athletic performance for Poomsae players.

Both the sensitivity of the muscular nervous system and the receptivity of the nerve signals delivered to the central nervous system are enhanced through balance training.

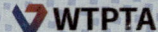

## 2. Poomsae specific functional exercises
### 공인품새를 위한 보강 운동

스포츠 전 종목이 모두 같은 형태의 보강 운동을 한다는 것은 기능적 특성을 고려하지 못한 비효율적인 트레이닝 방법이다. 스트레칭과 마찬가지로 태권도 품새 선수의 기능적 원리와 특성을 바탕으로 연구한 효율적인 보강 운동을 몇 가지 제시하려고 한다.

공인 품새를 위한 보강 운동을 상체, 코어, 하체, 밸런스 트레이닝 순으로 나열하였다.

### 태권도 품새 선수의 관절 별 안정성, 근력 강화 트레이닝의 필요성

기능적 안정성은 외부의 힘이나 변화가 있을 때, 몸의 정렬이 변형되지 않고 유지할 수 있는 능력을 말한다. 이는 몸의 인접한 부분을 신장하고 수축하는 동안 신체의 일부분을 안정되게 유지하며, 일관된 자세와 속도를 낼 수 있게 하기 때문에 품새 선수의 경기력 향상을 위해서는 필수라고 할 수 있다.

기능적 안정성을 향상시키려면 균형과 근육의 힘, 지구력, 이 3가지 요소가 모두 필요하다. 이는 강력한 퍼포먼스를 증진시키는 중요한 요소이기도 하다.

뒤에 나올 보강 운동은 관절 가동성과 함께 기능적 안정성, 근력의 기반을 확립하게 하여 품새 동작을 좀 더 정확하며 강하게 만들어 낼 수 있도록 도움을 줄 것이다.

### 태권도 품새 선수의 밸런스 트레이닝의 필요성

우리 몸의 밸런스 시스템은 대표적으로 시각계, 안뜰계, 몸감각계로 구성되어있다. 시각계, 안뜰계에 비해 고유수용성감각이 포함된 몸감각계는 생소할 것이다. 이를 쉽게 설명하자면, 관절의 위치를 의식적 혹은 무의식적으로 인식하는 것을 말하며, 근육, 힘줄, 인대 등에 있는 센서이다. 이는 움직임에 즉각 반응하여 올바르게 움직이고 균형을 잡을 수 있도록 한다. 따라서, 밸런스 능력이 중요한 품새 선수에게 고유수용성감각이란 경기력 향상에 필수적이며 중요하다고 할 수 있다.

뒤에 나올 밸런스 트레이닝을 통해 근 신경계의 민감도가 증가하여 신경계로 전달되는 운동 단위의 양이 많아지고, 고유수용성감각을 향상시켜 더 나아가 경기력 향상에 도움이 될 것이다.

# 2. Poomsae specific functional exercises
## 공인품새를 위한 보강 운동

### 1) Functional exercises of upper body (상체 보강 운동)

#### (1) No money

① Hold the band with your palm facing up and bend your elbows at 90 degrees to make the starting position.
② Externally rotate your shoulders and retract your scapulars.
③ Perform 20 repetitions for 3 sets in total.

① 밴드를 주먹 쥐어 잡고, 팔꿈관절을 90° 굽힘하여 준비자세를 만든다.
② 어깨뼈를 들임하며 어깨관절을 가쪽돌림한다.
③ 동작을 반복하여 20회씩 3세트 진행한다.

> Caution : Make sure your thumb is facing outward, and that your shoulders are level and not hunched. The band should be level with your belly button.
> Benefits : Strengthens the rhomboid muscle and rotator cuff.
> 주의사항 : 엄지방향이 바깥쪽을 향한 상태로 한다. 굽은 어깨 상태에서 하지 않는다. 밴드가 배꼽위치에 있게 한다.
> 효과 : 마름근, 어깨돌림근띠 강화.

#### (2) Rowing & elbow extension

① Hold the band with your palms facing inwards and bend your elbows at a 90 degrees to make the starting position.
② Retract your scapulars and extend your arms.
③ While maintaining scapular retraction, slowly bend your arms.
④ Perform 20 repetitions for 3 sets in total.

① 밴드를 주먹 쥐어 잡고, 팔꿈관절을 90° 굽힘하여 준비자세를 만든다.
② 어깨뼈를 들임하고 이를 유지하며 팔꿈관절을 편다.
③ 어깨뼈를 들임한 상태를 유지하고, 천천히 버티며 팔꿈관절만 굽힘한다.
④ 동작을 반복하여 20회씩 3세트 진행한다.

> Caution : Avoid hunching your shoulders. Maintain retraction of the shoulder blades.
> Benefits : Strengthens the rhomboid muscle, middle and lower trapezius, and upper arm triceps.
> 주의사항 : 굽은 어깨 상태에서 하지 않는다. 어깨뼈를 들임한 상태를 유지하며 한다.
> 효과 : 마름근, 중간·아래 등세모근, 위팔세갈래근 강화.

## 2. Poomsae specific functional exercises
## 공인품새를 위한 보강 운동

### (3) Cheerleader

① Hold the band with your hands and keep your arms straight in front of you to make the starting position.
② Externally rotate shoulders by retracting your scapulars.
③ Maintaining posture 2, raise one hand while lowering the other. Alternate hand positions.
④ Repeat steps 1-3 for one repetition. Perform 5 repetitions for 3 sets in total.

① 밴드를 주먹 쥐어 잡고, 팔꿈관절을 편 상태로 어깨관절을 90° 앞으로 굽힘하여 준비자세를 만든다.
② 어깨뼈를 들임하며 팔을 벌린다.
③ 2번 자세와 같이 대각선 2방향으로 팔을 벌린다.
④ 중앙, 대각선 좌, 우 3방향을 순서대로 반복하며 5바퀴씩 3세트 진행한다.

> **Caution :** Maintain retraction of the shoulder blades. Straighten your elbows. Do not overextend your arms to the back.
> **Benefits :** Strengthens the rhomboid muscle, middle and lower trapezius and upper arm triceps.
> 주의사항 : 어깨뼈를 들임, 팔꿈관절을 편 상태로 한다. 팔이 과하게 뒤로 넘어가지 않도록 한다.
> 효과 : 마름근, 중간·아래 등세모근, 위팔세갈래근 강화.

### (4) Horizontal external rotation

① Hold the band with your hand, bend your elbows at 90 degrees and raise your bent arm to the side to make the starting position. Your arm should be parallel to the floor.
② Externally rotate your shoulders.
③ Perform 20 repetitions for 3 sets in total.

① 밴드를 주먹 쥐어 잡고, 팔꿈관절 90° 굽힘, 어깨관절 90° 벌림하여 준비자세를 만든다.
② 1번 자세를 유지하며, 어깨 관절을 가쪽돌림한다.
③ 동작을 반복하여 20회씩 3세트 진행한다.

> **Caution :** Avoid hunching your shoulders. Do not overextend your arms to the back.
> **Benefits :** Strengthens rotator cuff and improves the strength of mountain block motion.
> 주의사항 : 굽은 어깨 상태에서 하지 않는다. 팔이 과하게 뒤로 넘어가지 않도록 한다.
> 효과 : 어깨돌림근띠 강화 및 산틀막기 안정성 향상.

## 2. Poomsae specific functional exercises
### 공인품새를 위한 보강 운동

### (5) Scaption

① Hold the band with your hands close to your legs while keeping your elbows straight to make the starting position.
② Raise your arms diagonally up to shoulder height.
③ Perform 20 repetitions for 3 sets in total.

① 밴드를 주먹 쥐어 잡고, 팔꿉관절을 편 상태로 준비자세를 만든다.
② 1번 자세를 유지하며, 어깨면(35°)에서 어깨관절을 굽힘한다.
③ 동작을 반복하여 20회씩 3세트 진행한다.

> Caution : Make sure that your thumbs are facing upward and that your scapulars are retracted.
> Benefits : Strengthens the deltoid muscle, upper trapezius, and upper triceps.
> 주의사항 : 몸통과 일자면이 아닌 어깨면(35°)에서 어깨뼈를 들임한 상태로 동작을 한다. 엄지방향이 위로 향하게 한다.
> 효과 : 어깨세모근, 위 등세모근, 위팔세갈래근 강화.

### (6) Shoulder press

① Hold the band with your hands, bend your elbows at 90 degrees, and raise your hands upward.
② Straighten your elbows, raising your arms up while pushing your hands upward.
③ Perform 20 repetitions for 3 sets in total.

① 밴드를 주먹 쥐어 잡고, 팔꿉관절 90° 굽힘, 어깨관절 90° 벌림하여 준비자세를 만든다.
② 팔꿉관절을 폄하면서 머리 위로 팔을 뻗는다.
③ 동작을 반복하여 20회 3세트 진행한다.

> Caution : Tighten your core to maintain back posture.
> Benefits : Strengthens the deltoid and pectoral muscles.
> 주의사항 : 허리가 과도하게 뒤로 젖혀지지 않도록 한다.
> 효과 : 어깨세모근, 큰가슴근 강화.

## 2. Poomsae specific functional exercises
## 공인품새를 위한 보강 운동

### (7) Shoulder touch & push up

① Make a push-up position while keeping your elbows straight. Make sure that your pelvis and spine form a straight line.
② Maintaining the first position, lift one hand to touch the opposite shoulder, then lift the other hand to touch the alternate shoulder.
③ Return to the first position, bend and extend your elbows to do one push-up.
④ Perform 20 repetitions for 3 sets in total.

① 엎드려 팔꿈관절을 편 상태에서 척주와 골반의 정렬을 맞춰 준비자세를 만든다.
② 1번 자세를 유지하며, 손을 바닥에서 떼어 어깨의 좌, 우를 한번씩 터치한다.
③ 1번 자세로 돌아와 팔꿈관절을 굽힘하고, 힘을 주어 바닥을 밀며 팔꿈관절을 편다.
④ 동작을 반복하여 20회씩 3세트 진행한다.

Caution : Maintain protraction of the scapulars. When touching your shoulder, fix your torso so that it does not rotate left or right.
Benefits : Strengthens the pectoralis major muscle, biceps brachii, triceps brachii. Improves shoulder stability.
주의사항 : 어깨뼈를 내밈한 상태를 유지한다. 어깨를 터치했을 때 몸통이 좌, 우로 틀어지지 않도록 버티며 한다.
효과 : 큰가슴근, 위팔두갈래근, 위팔세갈래근 강화 및 어깨 안정성 향상.

# 2. Poomsae specific functional exercises
## 공인품새를 위한 보강 운동

## 2) Functional exercises of core (코어 보강 운동)

### (1) Dead bug

① Lie on your back and raise your arms and bent legs upward to make the starting position.
② Lower one arm and extend the opposite leg at the same time while keeping your pelvis and spine on the floor by tightening your core.
③ Perform each movement in 10 seconds and do 10 repetitions for 3 sets in total.

① 등을 대고 누워, 어깨관절과 엉덩관절을 90°로 굽힘하여 준비자세를 만든다.
② 복부에 힘을 주어 척주와 골반을 바닥에 고정한 상태로 팔다리를 교차해 바닥 쪽으로 내린다.
③ 동작을 반복하여 10초씩 10회 3세트 진행한다.

> Caution : Tighten your core to prevent your back and waist from lifting up excessively.
> Benefits : Strengthens core stability.
> 주의사항 : 등과 허리가 과도하게 뜨지 않도록 코어에 힘을 유지한다.
> 효과 : 코어 안정성 강화.

### (2) Crunches

① Lie on your back and raise your legs to make the starting position.
② With your hands held in front of your body, bend your torso toward your legs using core strength.
③ Perform each movement in 5 seconds and do 20 repetitions for 3 sets in total.

① 등을 대고 누워, 다리를 들고 준비 자세를 만든다.
② 몸통에 손을 고정한 상태에서 코어의 힘으로 몸통을 굽힘한다.
③ 동작을 반복하여 5초씩 20회 3세트 진행한다.

> Caution : Do not bend your neck excessively. Do not bend your torso using the rebound force of your movement.
> Benefits : Strengthens core stability and core muscle strength.
> 주의사항 : 목을 과도하게 굽힘하지 않도록 한다. 반동으로 몸통을 굽힘하지 않는다.
> 효과 : 코어 안정성 및 근력 강화.

## 2. Poomsae specific functional exercises
### 공인품새를 위한 보강 운동

### (3) Cross spine twist

  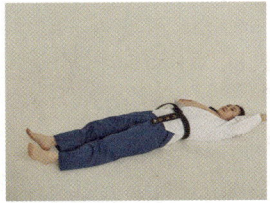 

① Start by laying with your back on the floor.
② Tighten your core and lift one arm and the opposite leg at the same time.
③ While bending your torso upward, twist your torso toward your leg by using your core strength.
④ Perform 20 repetitions for 3 sets in total.

① 바닥에 등을 대고 누워 준비 자세를 만든다.
② 복부에 힘을 주어 서로 교차되는 팔과 다리를 동시에 들어준다.
③ 이때 몸통을 비틀어 다리의 바깥쪽을 향해 몸통을 굽힘한다.
④ 동작을 반복하여 20회 3세트 진행한다.

Caution : Do not bend your torso using the rebound force of your movement.
Benefits : Strengthens core muscle strength.
주의사항 : 반동으로 몸통을 굽힘하지 않는다.
효과 : 코어 근력 강화.

### (4) Toe touch (3 directions)

① Lie on your back, raise your legs at 90 degrees, and straighten your arms towards your foot.
② Bend your upper body towards your toes. Return to the starting position, then bend your upper body diagonally to the left and right, respectively.
③ Perform 5 repetition for 5 sets in total.

① 등을 대고 누워 엉덩관절을 90°로 굽힘. 팔꿈관절을 편 준비자세를 만든다.
② 몸통을 굽힘하여 발가락, 왼쪽 복사뼈, 오른쪽 복사뼈 순서로 터치한다.
③ 동작을 반복하여 5바퀴 5세트 진행한다.

Caution : Only bend your upper body. Your lower body should be fixed. Do not bend your torso using the rebound force of your movement.
Benefits : Strengthens core muscle strength.
주의사항 : 하체는 고정한 채로 상체만 굽힘한다. 반동으로 몸통을 굽힘하지 않는다.
효과 : 코어 근력 강화.

## 2. Poomsae specific functional exercises
### 공인품새를 위한 보강 운동

### (5) Star plank

① Make a push-up position while keeping your elbows straight. Make sure that your pelvis and spine form a straight line.
② Tighten your core and lift one arm and the opposite leg at the same time. Alternate arms and legs.
③ Perform each movement for 5 seconds. Do 10 repetitions for 5 sets in total.

① 엎드려 팔꿉관절을 편 상태에서, 척추와 골반의 정렬을 맞춰 준비자세를 만든다.
② 복부에 힘을 유지한 채로 팔다리를 교차하여 든다.
③ 동작을 반복하여 5초씩 10회 5세트 진행한다.

> Caution : Do not twist your torso. Keep engaging your core.
> Benefits : Strengthens core stability and muscle strength.
> 주의사항 : 몸통이 틀어지지 않도록 한다. 코어에 긴장감을 유지한다.
> 효과 : 코어 안정성 및 근력 강화.

### (6) Dynamic plank

① Start with basic plank position and hold it for 10 seconds.
② Raise one arm and rotate your entire body to one side in a side plank position for 10 seconds.
③ Return to basic plank position for 10 seconds.
④ Make a side plank position on the other side for 10 seconds.
⑤ Perform 5 repetitions for 5 sets in total.

① 기본 플랭크로 준비 자세를 만들어 버틴다. (10초)
② 한쪽 팔을 들고 몸 전체를 회전하여 사이드 플랭크로 버틴다. (10초)
③ 다시 기본 플랭크로 버틴다. (10초)
④ 반대쪽도 몸 전체를 회전하여 사이드 플랭크로 버틴다. (10초)
⑤ 동작을 반복하여 5회 5세트 진행한다.

> Caution: Keep your core muscles engaged.
>          Make sure your spine is not twisted while maintaining plank position.
> Benefits : Strengthens core stability and muscle strength.
> 주의사항 : 코어근육에 긴장감을 유지한다.
>            기본 플랭크, 사이트 플랭크 모두 척추의 정렬을 유지하도록 한다.
> 효과 : 코어 안정성 및 근력 강화.

## 2. Poomsae specific functional exercises
### 공인품새를 위한 보강 운동

### (7) Mountain climber (2 directions)

    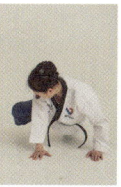 

① Make a push-up position while keeping your elbows straight. Make sure that your pelvis and spine form a straight line.
② Tighten your core, bend one knee outward and up toward the elbow.
③ Perform this motion with your alternate leg.
④ Repeat the movements quickly and perform 20 repetitions for 5 sets in total.

① 엎드려 팔꿈치관절을 편 상태에서, 척주와 골반의 정렬을 맞춰 준비자세를 만든다.
② 복부에 힘을 주고, 무릎관절을 굽힘하여 같은 방향으로 당겨온다.
③ 왼쪽과 오른쪽 번갈아 진행한다.
④ 빠르게 동작을 반복하여 20회 5세트 진행한다.

> Caution : Keep your core muscles engaged. Do not bend your neck excessively.
> Benefits : Strengthens core muscle strength.
> 주의사항 : 몸통의 무게 중심은 중앙에 두도록 한다. 목을 과도하게 굽힘하지 않도록 한다.
> 효과 : 코어 근력 강화.

### (8) Reverse dynamic plank

① Sit with your knees straight and your elbows straight to make the starting position.
② Lift your hips and hold this reverse plank position for 10 seconds.
③ Lift one leg in reverse plank position and hold it for 10 seconds.
④ Lift your alternate leg in reverse plank position and hold it for 10 seconds.
⑤ Perform 5 repetitions for 5 sets in total.

① 무릎관절을 폄하여 앉고, 팔꿈치관절을 폄하여 바닥을 지탱한 준비 자세를 만든다.
② 엉덩이를 들어 리버스 플랭크로 버틴다. (10초)
③ 왼쪽 다리를 들어 그대로 버틴다. (10초)
④ 반대인 오른쪽 다리를 들어 그대로 버틴다. (10초)
⑤ 동작을 반복하여 5회 5세트 진행한다.

> Caution : Do not twist your torso when you lift your legs. Keep engaging your core.
> Benefits : Strengthens core stability and muscle strength.
> 주의사항 : 다리를 드는 동작에도 몸통이 틀어지지 않도록 한다. 코어에 긴장감을 유지한다.
> 효과 : 코어 안정성 및 근력 강화.

# 2. Poomsae specific functional exercises
## 공인품새를 위한 보강 운동

### (9) Juchumseogi position & trunk rotation

① Hold the band with both hands while keeping your elbows straight in horse riding stance to make the starting position.
② Rotate your body and pull the band across your body.
③ Perform each movement for 5 seconds. Do 10 repetitions for 5 sets in total.

① 주춤서기에서 팔꿈관절을 편 상태로 밴드를 잡아 준비 자세를 만든다.
② 밴드 반대 방향으로 몸통을 회전한다.
③ 동작을 반복하여 5초씩 10회 5세트 진행한다.

> Caution : Keep your core engaged. Keep your lower body aligned and only rotate your torso.
> Benefits : Strengthens core strength and trunk rotation.
> 주의사항 : 코어에 긴장감을 유지한다. 하체의 정렬을 유지한 채, 몸통만 회전하도록 한다.
> 효과 : 코어 근력 및 몸통 회전력 강화.

### (10) Static lunge position & trunk rotation

① In a static lunge position, hold the band with both hands while keeping your elbows straight to make the starting position.
② Rotate your body and pull the band across your body.
③ Perform each movement for 5 seconds. Do 10 repetitions for 5 sets in total.

① 정적 런지 자세에서 팔꿈관절을 편 상태로 밴드를 잡아 준비 자세를 만든다.
② 밴드 반대 방향으로 몸통을 회전한다.
③ 동작을 반복하여 5초씩 10회 5세트 진행한다.

> Caution : Keep your core engaged. Keep your lower body aligned and only rotate your torso.
>           Rotate in the same direction as your front leg (i.e. if the right leg is in front, rotate to the right).
> Benefits : Strengthens core strength and trunk rotation.
> 주의사항 : 코어에 긴장감을 유지한다. 하체의 정렬을 유지한 채, 몸통만 회전하도록 한다.
>           다리와 같은 방향으로 회전한다. (오른쪽 다리가 앞에 위치하면 몸통을 오른쪽으로 회전한다)
> 효과 : 코어 근력 및 몸통 회전력 강화.

# 2. Poomsae specific functional exercises
## 공인품새를 위한 보강 운동

### 3) Functional exercises of lower body (하체 보강 운동)

#### (1) Standing terminal knee extension

① Put your band on one knee and lift your other leg to make the starting position.
② With your supporting leg bent at 30 degrees, slowly straighten your knee.
③ Perform each movement for 3 seconds. Do 20 repetitions for 5 sets in total.

① 밴드를 고정하여 묶은 뒤, 무릎에 걸고 한 다리로 서서 준비 자세를 만든다.
② 무릎관절이 30° 굽힘되어있는 상태에서 천천히 무릎관절을 펴며 힘을 준다.
③ 동작을 반복하여 3초씩 20회 5세트 진행한다.

> Caution : Do not bend your upper body while bending your knee.
> Benefits : Enhances patella stability and strengthens quadriceps.
> 주의사항 : 무릎관절을 굽힘할 때, 상체가 같이 숙여지지 않도록 한다.
> 효과 : 슬개골 안정성 및 대퇴사두근 강화.

#### (2) Hamstring walking

① Lie with your back on the floor and lift your hips to make a bridge as your starting position.
② Walk one step at a time in bridge position, while keeping your feet in dorsiflexion with your heels on the ground.
③ Walk away from your body for 2 steps, and walk back toward your body for 2 steps (stepping forward once with right and left foot counts as one step). Repeat for a total of 20 steps. Every 20 steps counts as 1 repetition.
④ Perform 3 repetition for 3 sets in total.

① 바닥에 등을 대고 누워 브릿지로 준비 자세를 만든다.
② 브릿지를 유지하며 발목의 발등굽힘을 유지한 상태로 한발씩 걷는다.
③ 한 발만 세웠을 때, 내려가는 2걸음 이어서 올라오는 2걸음, 총 20걸음 진행한다.
④ 동작을 반복하여 20걸음을 3회씩 3세트 진행한다.

> Caution : Maintain a bridge position throughout the walk. Avoid letting your waist drop.
> Benefits : Strengthens core stability and knee muscles.
> 주의사항 : 걷는 내내 브릿지 자세를 유지한다. 허리가 활처럼 휘어지지 않도록 한다.
> 효과 : 코어 안정성 및 뒤넙다리근 강화.

## 2. Poomsae specific functional exercises
### 공인품새를 위한 보강 운동

### (3) Back lunge & knee up

① Stand with your legs shoulder-width apart.
② Step back with one leg and lunge.
③ Without touching your knee on the floor, lift your back leg up to your chest, standing on on leg.
④ Perform each movement for 5 seconds. Do 20 repetitions for 5 sets in total.

① 다리를 어깨너비로 서서 준비 자세를 만든다.
② 한쪽 다리를 뒤로 빼서 동적 백 런지를 한다.
③ 그대로 뒤의 발을 끌어올려 한발로 서서 버틴다. (5초)
④ 동작을 반복하여 5초씩 20회 5세트 진행한다.

> Caution : Do not move quickly, rather slowly focus on muscle contraction. Do not lean back while lunging back.
> Benefits : Strengthens knee and hip joint stability, as well as muscle strength.
> 주의사항 : 동작을 빠르게 진행하지 않고, 천천히 근육 수축에 집중하여 진행한다. 동적 백 런지 시, 몸통이 뒤로 가지 않도록 한다.
> 효과 : 무릎·엉덩관절 안정성 및 근력 강화

### (4) Heel touch with step box (3 directions)

① Start by standing with one foot on the step box.
② Slowly bend the knee of your supporting leg.
③ Straighten your knee again after the heel of your non-supporting leg touches the floor.
④ Repeat step 2 and 3 touching the floor in front, on your side, and behind you, respectively, for 1 repetition.
⑤ Perform 5 repetitions for 5 sets in total.

① 스텝박스에 한 발로 서서 준비 자세를 만든다.
② 지지한 쪽의 무릎관절을 천천히 버티며 굽힘한다.
③ 지지하지 않은 쪽의 발꿈치로 앞의 바닥을 터치한 후, 올라온다.
④ 2번, 3번 자세를 반복하며, 지지하지 않은 쪽의 발꿈치로 앞, 중앙, 뒤 순서로 터치한다.
⑤ 동작을 반복하여 5바퀴씩 5세트 진행한다.

> Caution : Do not twist your pelvis when your heel touches the floor.
> Benefits : Strengthens the stability and strength of the ankle, knee, and hip joints.
> 주의사항 : 발꿈치를 바닥에 터치 할 때, 골반이 내려가며 틀어지지 않도록 한다.
> 효과 : 발목·무릎·엉덩관절 안정성 및 근력 강화

## 2. Poomsae specific functional exercises
## 공인품새를 위한 보강 운동

### (5) Dynamic lunge (3 directions)

① Start by standing with your legs shoulder-width apart.
② Step forward with one leg and lunge.
③ Return to standing position without your foot touching the floor, and land with your foot in front and diagonally inward to perform a cross lunge.
④ Return to standing position without your foot touching the floor, and land with your foot to the side to perform a side lunge.
⑤ Perform these 3 moves as 1 repetition. Do 5 repetitions for 5 sets in total.

① 다리를 어깨너비로 서서 준비 자세를 만든다.
② 한쪽 다리를 앞으로 빼어 동적 프론트 런지를 한다.
③ 그대로 앞의 발을 바닥에 닿지 않고 제자리로 돌아간 뒤, 이어 동적 크로스 런지를 한다.
④ 동일한 방법으로 이어서 동적 사이드 런지를 한다.
⑤ 이 3동작을 반복하여 5바퀴씩 5세트 진행한다.

> Caution : Do not move quickly, rather slowly focus on muscle elasticity.
>           Do not lean forward or twist your torso when doing the lunges.
> Benefits : Strengthens the stability and strength of the ankle, knee, and hip joints.
> 주의사항 : 동작을 빠르게 진행하지 않고, 천천히 근육 탄성에 집중하여 진행한다.
>            런지 시, 몸통을 과도하게 숙이지 않도록 한다.
> 효과 : 발목·무릎·엉덩관절 안정성 및 근력 강화.

### (6) Hip walking drill (10 directions)

① Tie a band around your ankles. Bend your knees into a mini squat at 30 degrees to make the starting position.
② Step with one foot to the front, front corner, side, back corner, and back, respectively. Repeat with the other foot for 1 repetition.
③ Perform 5 repetitions for 5 sets in total.

① 밴드를 묶어 발목에 걸고, 무릎관절을 30° 굽힌 미니 스쿼트로 준비 자세를 만든다.
② 왼발부터 앞, 앞-사선, 옆, 옆-사선, 뒤 순서대로 벌린다. 이어서 오른발도 동일하게 진행한다. (1바퀴)
③ 동작을 반복하여 5바퀴씩 5세트 진행한다.

> Caution : Do not bend your torso excessively. Maintain the center of your balance with your supporting foot. Do not bend your knee inwards.
> Benefits : Strengthens stability and muscle endurance of hip joints, knees and ankles. Improves the stability of your stance.
> 주의사항 : 몸통을 과도하게 숙이지 않도록 한다. 버티는 발은 몸통과 함께 정렬을 유지하며, 무릎이 안으로 들어가지 않도록 한다.
> 효과 : 엉덩·무릎·발목관절의 안정성 및 근지구력 강화, 서기의 안정화 향상.

## 2. Poomsae specific functional exercises
### 공인품새를 위한 보강 운동

### (7) Juchumseogi position & side walking

① Tie a band around your ankles with your legs bent and shoulder-width apart to make the starting position.
② Maintaining that posture, walk 10 steps to the right, and then 10 steps to the left for 1 lap.
③ Perform 5 laps for 5 sets in total.

① 밴드를 묶어 발에 걸고, 주춤서기로 준비자세를 만든다.
② 그대로 유지하며, 오른쪽으로 10걸음 걷고, 왼쪽으로 10걸음 걷는다. (1바퀴)
③ 이어서 5바퀴씩 5세트 진행한다.

Caution : Avoid moving your body up and down while performing your steps. Keep your body leveled.
Benefits : Strengthens stability and muscular endurance of hip joints, knees and ankles, improves the stability of your stance.
주의사항 : 과도하게 위, 아래로 움직이지 않도록 버티며 옆으로 걷는다.
효과 : 엉덩·무릎·발목관절의 안정성 및 근지구력 강화, 서기의 안정화 향상.

## 2. Poomsae specific functional exercises
## 공인품새를 위한 보강 운동

### 4) Functional exercises to improve balance (밸런스 보강 운동)

#### (1) Kettlebell T-balance with balance pad

① Start by standing with one foot on the balance pad and holding the kettlebell with both hands.
② Extend your non-supporting foot backward while lowering your upper body forward.
③ Make sure that your extended leg and your upper body form a straight line (T shape).
④ Perform each movement for 10 seconds. Do 5 repetitions for 5 sets in total.

① 밸런스 패드 위에 한 발로 서서 양손으로 케틀벨을 잡아 준비자세를 만든다.
② 지지하고 있는 발의 반대 발을 뒤로 뻗으며, 몸통이 함께 움직여 아래쪽으로 숙인다.
③ 이때 상체와 뒤로 뻗은 다리가 일직선 되도록 한다. (T자)
④ 동작을 반복하여 10초씩 5번 5세트 진행한다.

Caution : Avoid opening your pelvis while extending your leg. Choose a kettlebell with the right weight for you.
Benefits : Strengthens ankle stability and improving sense of balance, Effective in preventing hamstring injuries.
주의사항 : T자 자세를 유지할 때, 뒤로 뻗은 쪽의 골반이 열리지 않도록 고정한다. 본인에게 맞는 무게의 케틀벨을 선택한다.
효과 : 발목의 안정성 강화 및 균형감각 향상, 뒤넙다리근 부상 예방에 효과적.

#### (2) Kettlebell side T-balance with balance pad

① Start by standing with one foot on the balance pad in a side kick position. Hold the kettlebell in your rear hand.
② Raise your bent knee and push your pelvis forward.
③ Perform each movement for 10 seconds.
④ Do 5 repetition for 5 sets in total.

① 밸런스 패드 위에 옆차기 자세로 한 발로 선다.
② 한 손으로 케틀벨을 잡아 준비 자세를 만든다.
③ 천천히 골반을 밀어준다.
④ 동작을 반복하여 10초씩 5번 5세트 진행한다.

Caution : Do not twist your torso. Maintain tension in your core muscles.
Benefits : Strengthens ankle stability and improves sense of balance. Effective in preventing adductor muscle injuries.
주의사항 : 몸통이 돌아가지 않도록 수행한다. 코어근육에 긴장감을 유지한다.
효과 : 발목의 안정성 강화 및 균형감각 향상, 엉덩관절 모음근 부상 예방에 효과적.

## 2. Poomsae specific functional exercises
### 공인품새를 위한 보강 운동

### (3) Movements & Keumgangmakgi with balance pad

① Start by standing with the rear foot on the balance pad.
② From front stance with the rear foot on the balance pad, perform Hakdariseogi and Keumgangmakgi.
③ From riding horse stance, perform Hakdariseogi and Keumgangmakgi on the balance pad.
④ Perform 10 repetitions for 5 sets in total.

① 밸런스 패드에 두 발로 서서 준비 자세를 만든다.
② 앞굽이 후, 학다리서기, 금강막기를 실시한다.
③ 주춤서기 후, 학다리서기, 금강막기를 실시한다.
④ 동작을 반복하여 10회 5세트 진행한다.

> Caution : While maintaining your balance, perform the same movements as the actual Keumgangmakgi.
> Benefits : Strengthens knee and ankle stability. Improves the sense of balance.
>   Effective in minimizing mistakes during balance shift.
> 주의사항 : 균형 유지 시, 최대한 실제 상황이라고 생각하며 진행한다.
> 효과 : 무릎·발목관절의 안정성 강화 및 균형 감각 향상, 중심이동 시, 균형 유지 실수 최소화에 효과적.

### (4) 90° rotation of Hakdariseogi

① Start by standing on one foot and extending the other foot forward.
② Rotate your body 90° and simultaneously pull your extended foot in to perform Hakdriseogi and Keumgangmakgi.
③ Extend your foot again. Repeat step 2.
④ Repeat in all four directions for 1 lap.
⑤ Perform 3 laps for each set. Do 3 sets in total.

① 한 발은 지지하여 서고, 반대 발은 앞으로 뻗어준다.
② 뻗은 발을 끌어오는 것과 동시에 90° 회전하여 학다리서기, 금강막기를 실시한다.
③ 끌어온 발을 다시 뻗었다가 끌어오면서 90° 회전하여 학다리서기, 금강막기를 실시한다.
④ 4방향을 모두 실시하여 진행한다. (1바퀴)
⑤ 동작을 반복하여 3바퀴씩 5세트 진행한다.

> Caution : Make sure to rotate and pull in your extended leg into Hakdariseogi simultaneously.
> Benefits : Strengthens knee and ankle stability. Improves the sense of balance.
>   Effective in minimizing mistakes in Keumgang Poomsae.
> 주의사항 : 뻗은 발을 끌어옴과 동시에 회전해야 한다.
> 효과 : 무릎·발목관절의 안정성 강화 및 균형 감각 향상, 금강 품새에서의 실수 최소화에 효과적.

## 2. Poomsae specific functional exercises
## 공인품새를 위한 보강 운동

### (5) Dynamic lunge & Hakdariseogi (4 directions)

① Start by standing with your feet with shoulder-width apart.
② Step forward and do a dynamic lunge.
③ After lunging, pull back your front foot into Hakdariseogi.
④ Rotate 90° in that position and repeat step 2 and 3.
⑤ Repeat in all four directions for 1 lap.
⑥ Perform 3 laps for each set. Do 3 sets in total.

① 두발을 어깨너비로 서서 준비 자세를 만든다.
② 동적 프론트 런지를 한다.
③ 런지 후, 나간 발을 끌어와 학다리서기를 실시한다.
④ 그대로 축을 고정하고, 90°로 회전하며 동작을 반복한다.
⑤ 4방향 모두 시행한다. (1바퀴)
⑥ 3바퀴씩 5세트 진행한다.

**Caution** : When lunging, make sure that your knees do not lean too far forward than your foot.
**Benefits** : Strengthens knee and ankle stability. Improves the sense of balance.
Effective in minimizing mistakes during balance shift.
주의사항 : 런지 시, 무릎이 과도하게 발의 앞으로 나가지 않도록 한다.
효과 : 무릎·발목관절의 안정성 강화 및 균형 감각 향상, 중심이동 시, 균형 유지 실수 최소화에 효과적.

### (6) Side jump Hakdariseogi

① Standing with one foot, jump in a high parabolic motion and land with your other foot.
② As soon as you land, hold your balance and do Hakdariseogi stance.
③ Maintain your balance and perform Keumgangmakgi for 8 seconds.
④ Repeat the steps for the alternate foot. Each jump counts as 1 repetition.
⑤ Perform 10 repetitions for 5 sets in total.

① 한 발로 선 후, 옆으로 포물선을 그리며 높게 점프하여 착지한다.
② 착지하자마자 중심을 잡아주면서 학다리서기 자세를 만든다.
③ 중심을 잡으며 금강막기의 8초를 그대로 실시한다.
④ 한쪽씩 번갈아 점프하며 동작을 반복한다.
⑤ 10회 5세트 진행한다.

**Caution** : Ease the impact of your jump by landing gently.
**Benefits** : Strengthens knee and ankle stability. Improves the sense of balance.
Effective in minimizing mistakes in Keumgang Poomsae.
주의사항 : 점프 후 착지 시, 부드럽게 충격을 완화하며 착지한다.
효과 : 무릎·발목관절의 안정성 강화 및 균형 감각 향상, 금강 품새에서의 실수 최소화에 효과적.

## 2. Poomsae specific functional exercises
### 공인품새를 위한 보강 운동

### (7) Jump Hakdariseogi 4 directions

① Start in Hakdariseogi position.
② Rotate 90° while jumping, and land.
③ Hold your balance for 5 seconds after landing.
④ Repeat in all four directions for 1 lap.
⑤ Perform 3 laps for each set. Do 5 sets in total.

① 학다리자세로 준비 자세를 만든다.
② 90°로 회전하면서 점프 후, 착지한다.
③ 착지하여 균형을 잡는다. (5초)
④ 이어 4방향 모두 시행한다. (1바퀴)
⑤ 동작을 반복하여 3바퀴씩 5세트 진행한다.

Caution : Ease the impact of your jump by landing gently.
Benefits : Strengthens knee and ankle stability. Improves the sense of balance.
          Effective in minimizing mistakes in Keumgang Poomsae.
주의사항 : 점프 후 착지 시, 부드럽게 충격을 완화하며 착지한다.
효과 : 무릎·발목관절의 안정성 강화 및 균형 감각 향상, 금강 품새에서의 실수 최소화에 효과적.

# 3. Cool-down & static stretching
## 마무리 정적 스트레칭

### (1) Seated hamstring, adductor, quadratus lumborum stretching

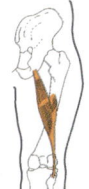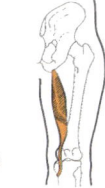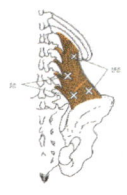

① Sit with one knee bent. Flex your feet in dorsiflexion with your hands.
② Bend your back and hold the posture for 20 seconds. Repeat with the other leg.
③ Repeat the motion by tilting the upper body sideways in the first position.

① 한쪽 무릎관절을 굽힘한 상태에서 반대쪽 무릎관절을 펴고 앉아,
   발목관절을 발등굽힘 상태로 만들어 손으로 고정한다.
② 손을 머리 위에 뻗어 고정한 후, 상체를 옆으로 기울인다.
③ 그 상태로 20초 동안 자세를 유지한 후, 반대쪽 방향을 실시한다.

> Caution : Make sure your hips stay in contact with the floor.
>           When your upper body is leaning to the side, fix your upper body so that it faces forward.
> 주의사항 : 골반이 바닥과 떨어지지 않도록 한다. 상체를 옆으로 기울인 자세에서는 상체가 앞을 보도록 고정한다.

### (2) Pigeon pose hip rotator stretching

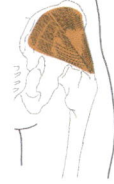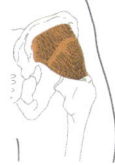

① From a seated position, bend your leading leg 90 degrees and externally rotate hip joint.
② Rotate your torso in the direction of your bent knee and lower your upper body.
③ After holding this posture for 20 seconds, perform with the other leg.

① 앉아서 한쪽 무릎관절을 90°로 굽힘하고, 엉덩관절을 가쪽돌림시켜 준비자세를 만든다.
② 구부린 무릎 방향으로 몸통을 회전시켜 골반을 밀어낸다.
③ 그 상태로 20초 동안 자세를 유지한 후, 반대쪽 방향을 실시한다.

> Caution : Push the pelvis in the direction of your calf and the floor. Do not bend your back excessively.
> 주의사항 : 골반을 반대 방향으로 밀어 넣어준다. 허리를 과하게 앞으로 숙이지 않도록 한다.

# 3. Cool-down & static stretching
## 마무리 정적 스트레칭

### (3) Half kneeling position psoas, quadriceps femoris stretching

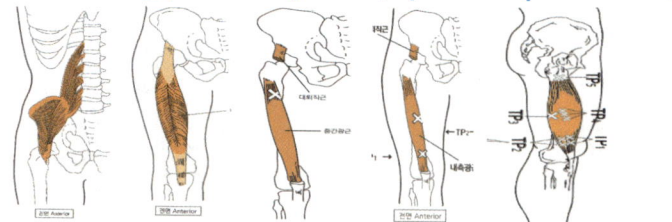

① Starting out in a position similar to long stance, drop your back knee onto the ground.
② Push your pelvis forward and hold for 20 seconds.
③ Grasp your back leg close to your ankle and continue pushing your hips forward.
④ After holding this posture for another 20 seconds, repeat with the other leg.

① 한쪽 무릎을 꿇은 상태에서 반대쪽의 무릎을 지면에 밀착시킨다.
② 앞에 세운 무릎을 앞으로 구부리며, 골반을 앞으로 밀어낸다.
③ 자세를 고정한 후, 손으로 뒤쪽 다리의 발목을 잡아당겨 무릎을 구부린다.
④ 그 상태로 20초 동안 자세를 유지한 후, 반대쪽 방향을 실시한다.

> Caution : Keep you pelvis aligned and keep your back straight. Ensure that your front leg does not tilt towards the inside of your body.
> 주의사항 : 골반이 좌, 우로 틀어지지 않도록 유지한다. 허리를 앞으로 숙이지 않도록 고정한다. 앞에 세운 다리가 과하게 안으로 들어가지 않도록 한다.

### (4) Standing erector spinae, quadratus lumborum, latissimus dorsi stretching

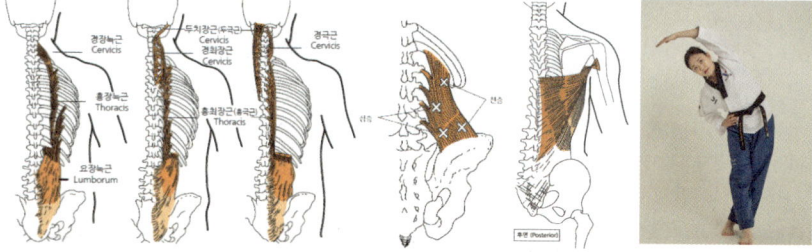

① While standing, put one leg to cross legs each other.
② Extend your arm upward and tilt your upper body to the side.
③ After holding the posture for 20 seconds in this position, perform in the opposite direction.

① 서서 한쪽 다리를 뒤로 꼬아 고정한다.
② 손을 머리 위에 뻗어 고정한 후, 상체를 옆으로 기울인다.
③ 그 상태로 20초 동안 자세를 유지한 후, 반대쪽 방향을 실시한다.

> Caution : Keep your legs parallel and shift your weight with your pelvis.
> 주의사항 : 두 다리가 11자가 되도록 한다. 골반과 함께 중심 이동을 해야 한다.

# III

## Poomsae

(공인품새)

# Taegeuk 1 Jang
## 태극 1장

Taegeuk 1 Jang represents the symbol Geon of Palgwe, one of the eight divination signs. The eight divination signs consist of Geon, Tae, Yi, Jin, Son, Gam, Gan, and Gon. The trigram Geon is associated with Yang or heaven and the begining of all creation in the universe. Similarly, Taegeuk 1 Jang represents the beginning in the training of Taekwondo. This Poomsae consists of basic blocks, strikes, stances and kicks such as Are Makgi (low block), Momtong Anmakgi (inward block), Momtong Jireugi (punch) and Apchagi (front kick), and is characterized by its ease of practice.
(Kukkiwon, 2022).
Shape of Poomsae : 王
Number of Poom : 18

태극 1장은 팔괘의 건(建)을 의미하며 건은 하늘과 양(陽)을 뜻한다. 건이 만물의 근원이 되는 시초를 나타낸 것과 같이 태권도에 있어서 맨 처음의 품새이다. 특징은 서기에서는 가장 쉬운 걷기 위주 동작이며 동작은 기초적인 몸통막기, 몸통지르기, 앞차기로 구성되어 있다(국기원, 2022).
품새선 : 王
품수 : 18품

# Taegeuk 1 Jang
# 태극 1장

Kibon Junbiseogi

기본 준비

1. Turn to the left, making a walking stance with your left foot forward and a left hand low block.

1. 왼발 왼쪽으로 내디뎌 앞서기 왼 아래막기

2. Step forward into a walking stance with your right foot forward with a right hand punch.

2. 오른발 내디뎌 앞서기 오른 몸통지르기

3. Step back with your right foot and turn 180° to the right, making a right leg walking stance and a right hand low block.

3. 오른쪽으로 돌아 오른 앞서기 오른 아래막기

4. Step forward into a left leg walking stance with a left hand punch.

4. 왼발 내디뎌 앞서기 왼 몸통지르기

5. Turn left toward the front and step forward into a left leg long stance with a left hand low block.

5. 왼발 왼쪽으로 내디뎌 앞굽이 왼 아래막기

World class Poomsae guide book

# Taegeuk 1 Jang
# 태극 1장

6. Keeping your stance, punch with your right hand.

6. 발자세 그대로 오른 몸통지르기

7. Turn toward the right and step forward into a right leg walking stance with a left hand chest block.

7. 오른발 오른쪽으로 내디뎌 앞서기 왼 안막기

8. Step forward, into a left leg walking stance with a right hand punch.

8. 왼발 내디뎌 앞서기 오른 몸통지르기

9. Step back with your left foot and turn 180° to the left, making a left leg walking stance and a right hand chest block.

9. 왼쪽으로 돌아 왼 앞서기 오른 안막기

10. Step forward into a right leg walking stance with a left hand punch.

10. 오른발 내디뎌 앞서기 왼 몸통지르기

11. Turn right toward the front and step forward into a right leg long stance with a right hand low block.

11. 오른발 오른쪽으로 내디뎌 앞굽이 오른 아래막기

# Taegeuk 1 Jang
# 태극 1장

12. Keeping your stance, punch with your left hand.

12. 발자세 그대로 왼 몸통지르기

13. Turn toward the left and step forward into a left leg walking stance with a left hand high block.

13. 왼발 왼쪽으로 내디뎌 앞서기 왼 얼굴막기

14. Front kick with your right leg, landing forward in a right leg walking stance with a right hand punch.

14. 오른발 앞차고 오른 앞서기 오른 몸통지르기

15. Step back with your right foot and turn 180° to the right, making a right leg walking stance and a right hand high block.

15. 오른쪽으로 돌아 오른 앞서기 오른 얼굴막기

16. Front kick with your left leg, landing forward in a left leg walking stance with a left hand punch.

16. 왼발 앞차고 왼 앞서기 왼 몸통지르기

# Taegeuk 1 Jang
# 태극 1장

17. Turn right toward the back and step forward into a left leg long stance with a left hand low block.

17. 왼발 오른쪽으로 내디뎌 앞굽이 왼 아래막기

18. Step forward into a right leg long stance with a right hand punch with Kihap.

18. 오른발 내디뎌 앞굽이 오른 몸통지르기(기합)

Baro
바로

Important movements: Are Makgi (low block), Momtong Anmakgi (inward blcok), Eolgul Makgi (high block), Momtong Jireugi (middle section punch)
Important Stances: Apseogi (walking stance), Apgubi (long stance).

# Taegeuk 2 Jang
# 태극 2장

Taegeuk 2 Jang represents the symbol Tae of Palgwe. The trigram Tae signifies inner firmness and outler softness like a lake. With the practice of Taegeuk 2 Jang, one develops a strong understanding of Poomsae as well as basic blocking and kicking. A technique that is introduced in this Poomsae is Eolgul Jireugi (high punch). Multiple front kicks are incorporated in Taegeuk 2 Jang to build front kick skill and strength.(Kukkiwon, 2022).

Shape of Poomsae: 王
Number of Poom: 18

태극 2장은 팔괘의 태(兌)를 의미하며 속으로 단단하고 겉으로는 부드럽고, 수면은 고요하나 수심이 깊은 연못과 같은 외유내강을 뜻한다. 태극 2장을 수련하면 품새에 대한 알찬 마음이 생겨 기초적인 막기와 차기를 할 수 있다. 새로운 동작은 얼굴지르기이며 앞차기 동작을 많이 넣어 몸에 익히게 하였다(국기원, 2022).

품새선 : 王
품수 : 18품

# Taegeuk 2 Jang
# 태극 2장

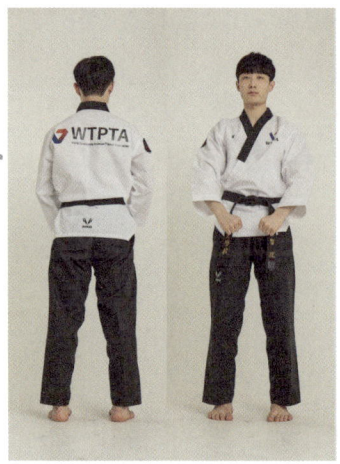

Kibon Junbiseogi

기본 준비

1. Turn to the left, making a walking stance with your left foot forward and a left hand low block.

1. 왼발 왼쪽으로 내디뎌 앞서기
   왼 아래막기

2. Step forward into a long stance with your right foot forward with a right hand punch.

2. 오른발 내디뎌 앞굽이
   오른 몸통지르기

3. Step back with your right foot and turn 180° to the right, making a right leg walking stance and a right hand low block.

3. 오른쪽으로 돌아 오른 앞서기
   오른 아래막기

4. Step forward into a left leg long stance with a left hand punch.

4. 왼발 내디뎌 앞굽이 왼 몸통지르기

5. Turn left toward the front and step forward with your left foot into a left leg walking stance with a right hand chest block.

5. 왼발 왼쪽으로 내디뎌 앞서기
   오른 안막기

# Taegeuk 2 Jang
## 태극 2장

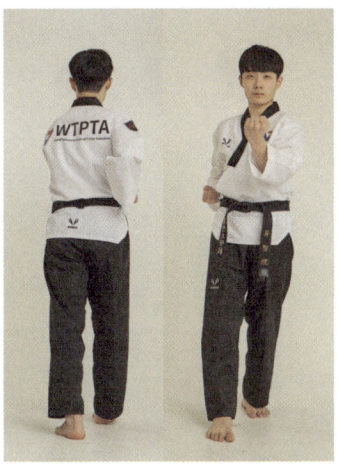

6. Step forward into a right leg walking stance with a left hand chest block.

6. 오른발 내디뎌 앞서기 왼 안막기

7. Turn toward the left and step forward with your left foot into a left leg walking stance with a left hand low block.

7. 왼발 왼쪽으로 내디뎌 앞서기 왼 아래막기

8. Front kick with your right leg, landing forward in a right leg long stance with a right hand high punch.

8. 오른발 앞차고 오른 앞굽이 오른 얼굴지르기

9. Step back with your right foot and turn 180° to the right, making a right leg walking stance and a right hand low block.

9. 오른쪽으로 돌아 오른 앞서기 오른 아래막기

10. Front kick with your left leg, landing forward in a left leg long stance with a left hand high punch.

10. 왼발 앞차고 왼 앞굽이 왼 얼굴지르기

# Taegeuk 2 Jang
## 태극 2장

11. Turn left toward the front and step forward with your left foot into a left leg walking stance with a left hand high block.

11. 왼발 왼쪽으로 내디뎌 앞서기 왼 얼굴막기

12. Step forward into a right leg walking stance with a right hand high block.

12. 오른발 내디뎌 앞서기 오른 얼굴막기

13. Turn to the left and step forward with your left foot into a left leg walking stance with a right hand chest block.

13. 왼쪽으로 돌아 왼 앞서기 오른 안막기

14. Turn 180° to the right, making a right leg walking stance and a left hand chest block.

14. 오른쪽으로 돌아 오른 앞서기 왼 안막기

15. Turn left toward the back and step forward with your left foot into a left leg walking stance and a left hand low block.

15. 왼발 왼쪽으로 내디뎌 앞서기 왼 아래막기

# Taegeuk 2 Jang
# 태극 2장

16. Front kick with right leg, landing forward in a right leg walking stance with a right hand punch.

16. 오른발 앞차고 오른 앞서기 오른 몸통지르기

17. Front kick with your left leg, landing forward in a left leg walking stance with a left hand punch.

17. 왼발 앞차고 왼 앞서기 왼 몸통지르기

18. Front kick with your right leg, landing forward in a right leg walking stance with a right hand punch with Kihap.

18. 오른발 앞차고 오른 앞서기 오른 몸통지르기(기합)

World class Poomsae guide book 55

# Taegeuk 2 Jang
## 태극 2장

Baro
바로

Important movements: Are Makgi (low block), Momtong Anmakgi (chest block), Ulgul Makgi (high block), Momtong Jireugi (punch).
Important Stances: Apseogi (walking stance), Apgubi (long stance).

# Taegeuk 3 Jang
## 태극 3장

Taegeuk 3 Jang represents the symbol Yi of Palgwe one of the eight divination signs. The eight divination signs consist of Geon, Tae, Yi, Jin, Son, Gam, Gan, and Gon The trigram Yi means "hot" and "bright" like the sun. Its significance encourages the trainees to develop courageous mindset and passion for training. Techniques that are introduced in this Poomsae are Mok Sonal Anchigi (inward knife hand neck strike), Sonal Bakkanmakgi (outward single knife hand block) and Dwitgubi (back stance). Taegeuk 3 Jang is characterized by blocks, kicks, punches and successive punches. This Poomsae involves techniques that quickly block and defeat the opponent's attacks, where strength is a critical skill.(Kukkiwon, 2022).
Shape of Poomsae: 王
Number of Poom: 20

태극 3장은 팔괘의 이(離)를 의미하며 이는 태양과 같은 뜨겁고 밝음을 의미한다. 태권도 품새 수련을 통한 불같은 정의심과 수련의욕이 생겨나 파란띠로 승급 할 수 있는 과정이다.
새로운 동작은 한손날비틀어목치기, 한손날몸통바깥막기, 새로운 서기는 뒷굽이이며, 기술은 연속 막고 지르기와 차고 연속 지르기가 특성이다. 빠른 속도로 상대로부터 공격을 막고 받아치는 기술의 힘을 중요시 한다(국기원, 2022).
품새선 : 王
품수 : 20품

The picture only shows the last punch instead of both of the punches.
지면관계상 두번지르기는 마지막 동작만 실었다.

# Taegeuk 3 Jang
## 태극 3장

Kibon Junbiseogi

기본 준비

1. Turn to the left, making a left leg walking stance and a left hand low block.

1. 왼발 왼쪽으로 내디뎌 앞서기 왼 아래막기

2. Front kick with your right leg, landing forward in a right leg long stance with a double punch (right, then left hand punch in succession).

2. 오른발 앞차고 오른 앞굽이 두 번 지르기(오른-왼)

3. Step back with your right foot and turn 180° to the right, making a right leg walking stance and a right hand low block.

3. 오른쪽으로 돌아 오른 앞서기 오른 아래막기

4. Front kick with your left leg, landing forward in a left leg long stance with a double punch (left, then right hand punch in succession).

4. 왼발 앞차고 왼 앞굽이 두 번 지르기(왼-오른)

# Taegeuk 3 Jang
## 태극 3장

5. Turn left toward the front and step forward into a left leg walking stance with a right inward knife hand neck strike.

5. 왼발 왼쪽으로 내디뎌 앞서기 오른 손날안치기

6. Step forward into a right leg walking stance with a left inward knife hand neck strike.

6. 오른발 내디뎌 앞서기 왼 손날안치기

7. Turn toward the left and step forward into a back stance with your left foot forward with a left outer single knife hand block.

7. 왼발 왼쪽으로 내디뎌 뒷굽이 왼 손날바깥막기

8. Slightly step forward with your left foot into a left leg long stance with a right hand punch.

8. 왼발 내디뎌 앞굽이 오른 몸통지르기

9. Turn 180° to the right, making a back stance with your right foot forward and a right outer single knife hand block.

9. 오른쪽으로 돌아 왼 뒷굽이 오른 손날바깥막기

# Taegeuk 3 Jang
# 태극 3장

10. Slightly step forward with your right foot into a right leg long stance with a left hand punch.

10. 오른발 내디뎌 앞굽이 왼 몸통지르기

11. Turn left toward the front and step forward into a left leg walking stance with a right hand inward chest block.

11. 왼발 왼쪽으로 내디뎌 앞서기 오른 몸통안막기

12. Step forward into a right leg walking stance and a left hand inward chest block.

12. 오른발 내디뎌 앞서기 왼 몸통안막기

13. Turn 270° to the left and step forward with your left foot into a left leg walking stance with a left hand low block.

13. 왼쪽으로 돌아 왼 앞서기 왼 아래막기

14. Front kick with your right leg, landing forward in a right leg long stance with a double punch (right, then left hand punch in succession).

14. 오른발 앞차고 오른 앞굽이 두 번 지르기(오른-왼)

# Taegeuk 3 Jang
# 태극 3장

15. Step back with your right foot and turn 180° to the right, making a right leg walking stance and a right hand low block.

15. 오른쪽으로 돌아 오른 앞서기 오른 아래막기

16. Front kick with your left leg, landing forward in a left leg long stance with a double punch (left, then right hand punch in succession).

16. 왼발 앞차고 왼 앞굽이 두 번 지르기(왼-오른)

17. Turn left toward the back and step forward into a left leg walking stance with a left hand low block, followed by a right hand punch.

17. 왼발 왼쪽으로 내디뎌 앞서기 왼 아래막고 오른 몸통지르기

18. Step forward into a right leg walking stance with a right hand low block, followed by a left hand punch.

18. 오른발 내디뎌 앞서기 오른 아래막고 왼 몸통지르기

# Taegeuk 3 Jang
# 태극 3장

19. Front kick with your left leg, landing forward in a left leg walking stance with left hand low block, followed by a right hand punch.

19. 왼발 앞차고 왼 앞서기
    왼 아래막고 오른 몸통지르기

20. Front kick with your left leg, landing forward in a right leg walking stance with right hand low block, followed by a left hand punch with Kihap.

20. 오른발 앞차고 오른 앞서기
    오른 아래막고 왼 몸통지르기(기합)

# Taegeuk 3 Jang
# 태극 3장

Baro
바로

Important movements: Mok Sonnal Anchigi(inward knife hand neck strike), Sonnal Bakkanmakgi(outward single knife hand block), double Jireugi (double punch)
Important Stance: Dwitgubi (back stance)

# Taegeuk 4 Jang
## 태극 4장

Taegeuk 4 Jang represents the symbol Jin of Palgwe. The trigram Jin is associated with thunder, signifying a dragon which contains great power and dignity. Techniques that are introduced in this Poomsae are Sonnal Geodeuro Bakkanmakgi (supported outward knife hand block), Pyeonsonkeut Sewojjireugi (supported upright thrust), Jebipum Anchigi (swallow-shaped strike), Yeop Chagi (side kick), Momtong Bakkanmakgi (outward middle block), Deungjumeok Apchigi (forward back fist strike to the face). Taegeuk 4 Jang is characterized by its many back stances and its various movements that prepares one for sparring.(Kukkiwon, 2022).
Shape of Poomsae: 王
Number of Poom: 20

태극 4장은 팔괘의 진(震)을 의미하며 진은 천둥과 번개를 나타내고 위엄있는 용(龍)을 뜻한다.
새로운 동작은 손날바깥막기, 거들어세워찌르기, 제비품안치기, 옆차기, 바깥막기, 등주먹앞치기가 있다. 겨루기에 대비한 각종 동작과 뒷굽이 서기가 많다는 것이 특징이다(국기원, 2022).
품새선 : 王
품수 : 20품

# Taegeuk 4 Jang
## 태극 4장

Kibon Junbiseogi

기본 준비

1. Turn to the left, making a back stance with your left foot forward and a left supported outward knife hand block.

1. 왼발 왼쪽으로 내디뎌 뒷굽이 손날거들어바깥막기

2. Step forward into a right leg long stance with a right supported upright thrust.

2. 오른발 내디뎌 앞굽이 오른 거들어 세워 찌르기

3. Step back with your right foot and turn 180° to the right, making a back stance with your right foot forward and a right supported outward knife hand block.

3. 오른쪽으로 돌아 왼 뒷굽이 손날거들어바깥막기

4. Step forward into a left leg long stance with a left supported upright thrust.

4. 왼발 내디뎌 앞굽이 왼 거들어세워찌르기

5. Turn left toward the front and step forward into a left leg long stance with swallow-shaped strike (left open hand high block and right knife hand neck strike).

5. 왼발 왼쪽으로 내디뎌 앞굽이 제비품안치기(목높이)

# Taegeuk 4 Jang
# 태극 4장

6. Front kick with your right leg, landing forward in a right leg long stance with a left hand punch.

6. 오른발 앞차고 오른 앞굽이 왼 몸통지르기

7-8. Side kick with your left leg, landing forward in a left leg walking stance. Side kick with your right leg, landing forward in a back stance with your right leg forward with a right supported outward knife hand block.

7-8. 왼발 옆차고 오른발 옆차고 왼 뒷굽이 손날바깥막기

9. Turn 270° to the left and step forward with your left foot into a back stance with your left leg forward with a left hand outward middle block.

9. 왼쪽으로 돌아 오른 뒷굽이 왼 바깥막기

# Taegeuk 4 Jang
# 태극 4장

10. Front kick with your right foot, landing back in a back stance with your left foot forward with a right hand inward chest block.

10. 오른발 앞차고 오른 뒷굽이 오른 안막기

11. Turn 180° to the right, making a leg back stance with your right foot forward and a right hand outward middle block.

11. 오른쪽으로 돌아 왼 뒷굽이 오른 바깥막기

12. Front kick with your left leg, landing back in a back stance with your left leg forward with a left hand inward chest block.

12. 왼발 앞차고 왼 뒷굽이 왼 안막기

13. Turn left toward the back and step forward into a left leg long stance with a swallow-shaped strike (left open hand high block and right knife hand neck strike).

13. 왼쪽으로 내디뎌 앞굽이 제비품안치기(목높이)

World class Poomsae guide book  67

# Taegeuk 4 Jang
# 태극 4장

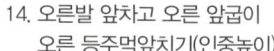

14. Front kick with your right leg, landing forward in a right leg long stance with a right hand back fist forward face strike

14. 오른발 앞차고 오른 앞굽이 오른 등주먹앞치기(인중높이)

15-16. Turn to the left and step forward into a left leg walking stance with a left hand inward chest block, followed by a right hand punch.

15-16. 왼발 왼쪽으로 내디뎌 앞서기 왼 안막고 오른 몸통지르기

17-18. Turn 180° to the right, making a right leg walking stance and a right hand inward chest block, followed by a left hand punch.

17-18. 오른쪽으로 돌아 오른 앞서기 오른 안막고 왼 몸통지르기

# Taegeuk 4 Jang
# 태극 4장

19. Turn left toward the back and step forward into a left leg long stance with a left hand inward chest block, followed by a double punch (left, then right hand punch in succession).

19. 왼발 왼쪽으로 내디뎌 앞굽이 왼 안막고 두 번 지르기(오-왼)

20. Step forward into a right leg long stance with a right hand inward chest block, followed by a double punch (right, then left hand punch in succession) with Kihap.

20. 오른발 내디뎌 앞굽이 오른 안막고 두 번 지르기(완-오)(기합)

Baro
바로

Important movements: Sonnal Bakkanmakgi (supported outward knife hand block), Pyeonsonkeut Sewojireugi (supported upright thrust), Momtong Bakkanmakgi (outward middle block), Yeop Chagi (side kick), Deungjumeok Apchigi (back fist forward face strike)

# Taegeuk 5 Jang
## 태극 5장

Taegeuk 5 Jang represents the symbol Son of Palgwe, The trigram Son is associated with the wind and has characteristics of both mighty force and calmness, just as this Poomsae emphasises relaxation and tensions and the flow of movements. Techniques that are newly introduced in this Poomsae are Mejumeok Naeryeochigi (downward hammer fist strike), Palggumchi Dollyeochigi (supported turning elbow strike to the face) supported turning elbow strike to the face Mejumeok Yeopchigi (hammer fist strike to the side), Palggumchi Pyojeokchigi (elbow target strike), Kkoaseogi (cross stance), Oen Seogi (left L-stance), Oreun Seogi (right L-stance).(Kukkiwon, 2022).
Shape of Poomsae: 王
Number of Poom: 20

팔괘의 손(巽)을 의미하며 손은 바람을 나타내고 위세와 고요의 뜻을 지닌다. 힘을 다양하게 발휘하도록 수련하는 과정을 뜻한다.
새로운 동작은 메주먹내려치기, 팔꿈치 거들어 돌려치기, 메주먹옆치기, 팔꿈치 표적앞치기가 있고, 서기는 꼬아서기와 왼서기, 오른서기가 나온다. 특징으로는 차기 뒤에 아래막고 몸통막기를 하는 연속되는 동작과 뛰어 구르면서 치는 동작이 특수하고, 표적치기 시에는 표적이 움직이지 않게 주의해야 한다(국기원, 2022).
품새선 : 王
품수 : 20품

# Taegeuk 5 Jang
## 태극 5장

Kibon Junbiseogi

기본 준비

1. Turn to the left, making a left leg long stance and a left hand low block.

1. 왼발 왼쪽으로 내디뎌 앞굽이 왼 아래막기

2. Slide your left leg back into a left L-stance with a left downward hammer fist strike.

2. 왼발 당겨 왼서기 왼 메주먹 내려치기

3. Turn 180° to the right, making a right leg long stance and a right hand low block.

3. 오른쪽으로 돌아 오른 앞굽이 오른 아래막기

4. Slide your right leg back into a right leg L-stance with a right downward hammer fist strike.

4. 오른발 당겨 오른서기 오른 메주먹 내려치기

5. Turn left toward the front and step forward into a left leg long stance with a left hand inward chest block, followed by a right hand inward chest block.

5. 왼발 왼쪽으로 내디뎌 앞굽이 왼 안막고 오른 안막기

# Taegeuk 5 Jang
# 태극 5장

6. Front kick with your right leg, landing forward in a right leg long stance with a right hand back fist forward face strike followed by a left hand inward chest block.

6. 오른발 앞차고 오른 앞굽이 오른 등주먹 앞치고(인중높이) 왼 안막기

7. Front kick with your left leg, landing forward in a left leg long stance with a left hand back fist forward face strike followed by a right hand inward chest block.

7. 왼발 앞차고 왼 앞굽이 왼 등주먹 앞치고 (인중높이) 오른 안막기

# Taegeuk 5 Jang
## 태극 5장

8. Step forward into a right leg long stance with a right hand back fist forward face strike

8. 오른발 내디뎌 앞굽이 오른 등주먹 앞치기(인중높이)

9. Turn 270° to the left and step forward into a back stance with your left foot forward with a left outward single knife hand block.

9. 왼쪽으로 돌아 오른 뒷굽이 왼 손날 바깥막기

10. Step forward into a right leg long stance with a supported right turning elbow strike to the face

10. 오른발 내디뎌 앞굽이 오른 팔꿈치 거들어 돌려치기

11. Step back with your right foot and turn 180° to the right, making a back stance with your right foot forward with a right outward single knife hand block.

11. 오른쪽으로 돌아 왼 뒷굽이 오른 손날 바깥막기

12. Step forward into a left leg long stance and a supported left turning elbow strike to the face

12. 왼발 내디뎌 앞굽이 왼 팔꿈치 거들어 돌려치기

# Taegeuk 5 Jang
## 태극 5장

13. Turn left toward the back and step forward with your left foot into a left leg long stance with a left leg long stance, followed by a right hand low block.

13. 왼발 왼쪽으로 내디뎌 앞굽이 왼 아래막고 오른 안막기

14. Front kick with your right leg, landing forward in a right leg long stance with a right hand low block, followed by a left hand inward chest block.

14. 오른발 앞차고 오른 앞굽이 오른 아래막고 왼 안막기

15. Turn to the left and step forward into a left leg long stance with a left hand high block.

15. 왼발 왼쪽으로 내디뎌 앞굽이 왼 얼굴막기

# Taegeuk 5 Jang
# 태극 5장

16. Right leg side kick with a right hammer fist strike to the side, landing forward in a right leg long stance with a left elbow target strike.

16. 오른발 옆차기와 동시에 오른 메주먹옆치고 내디뎌 오른 앞굽이 왼 팔꿈치 표적 앞치기

17. Step back with your right foot and turn 180° to the right, making a right leg long stance and a right hand high block.

17. 오른쪽으로 돌아 오른 앞굽이 오른 얼굴막기

18. Left leg side kick with a left hammer fist strike to the side, landing forward in a left leg long stance with a right elbow target strike.

18. 왼발 옆차기와 동시에 왼 메주먹옆치고 내디뎌 왼 앞굽이 오른 팔꿈치 표적 앞치기

19. Turn left toward the back and step forward with your left foot in a left leg long stance with a left hand low block, followed by a right hand inward chest block.

19. 왼발 왼쪽으로 내디뎌 앞굽이 왼 아래막고 오른 안막기

World class Poomsae guide book 75

# Taegeuk 5 Jang
## 태극 5장

20. Front kick with your right leg, landing the distance of one long stance forward with a stomp in a right foot cross stance with your toes pointed left. As you land, right hand back fist forward face strike with Kihap.

20. 오른발 앞차고 짓찧으며 꼬아서기 오른 등주먹 앞치기(인중높이, 기합)

Baro
바로

Important movements: Mejumeok Naeryeochigi (downward hammer fist strike), Palggumchi Dollyeochigi (supported turned elbow strike to the face), Palggumchi Pyojeokchigi (elbow target strike), side kick with Mejumeok Yeopchigi (side kick with hammer fist strike to the side)
Important stances: Oen Seogi (left L-stance), Oreun Seogi (right L-stance), Kkoaseogi (cross stance)

# Taegeuk 6 Jang
## 태극 6장

Taegeuk 6 Jang represents the symbol Gam of Palgwe. The trigram Gam is associated with water, signifying a continuous flow and softness. Like the characteristics of water, which is the life source of all things, the movement of the techniques performed in this Poomsae should flow like water. Techniques that are introduced in this Poomsae are Sonnal Eolgul Biteureomakgi (outward twisted knife hand face block), Dollye Chagi (roundhouse kick), Eolgul Bakkanmakgi (outward face block), Arae Hecheomakgi (low scatter block), Batangson Anmakgi (inward palm block). (Kukkiwon, 2022).
Shape of Poomsae: 王
Number of Poom: 19

태극 6장은 팔괘의 감(坎)을 의미하며 감은 물을 나타내고 끊임없는 흐름과 유연함을 뜻한다. 물의 특성처럼 기술이 흐르듯이 연결되어야 한다.
새로운 동작은 얼굴 손날 비틀어 바깥막기, 돌려차기, 얼굴바깥막기, 아래헤쳐막기, 바탕손안막기가 나온다. 수련상의 유의점은 돌려차고 난 다음 찬 발을 정확히 앞으로 내딛기와 바탕손안막기를 할 때는 막는 부위가 다르므로 팔목으로 막을 때보다 손바닥 길이만큼 낮추어야 한다. (국기원, 2022).
품새선 : 王
품수 : 19품

# Taegeuk 6 Jang
## 태극 6장

Kibon Junbiseogi

기본 준비

1. Turn to the left, making a left leg long stance and a left hand low block.

1. 왼발 왼쪽으로 내디뎌 앞굽이 왼 아래막기

2. Front kick with your right leg, landing back in a back stance with your left foot forward with a left outward middle block.

2. 오른발 앞차고 오른 뒷굽이 왼 바깥막기

3. Turn 180° to the right, making a right leg long stance and a right hand low block.

3. 오른쪽으로 돌아 오른 앞굽이 오른 아래막기

4. Front kick with your left leg, landing back in a back stance with your right foot forward with a right outward middle block.

4. 왼발 앞차고 왼 뒷굽이 오른 바깥막기

# Taegeuk 6 Jang
# 태극 6장

5. Turn left toward the front and step forward with your left foot into a left leg long stance with a right outward twisted knife hand face block.

5. 왼발 왼쪽으로 내디뎌 앞굽이 오른 얼굴 손날 비틀어 바깥막기

6. Right leg roundhouse kick, landing the distance of one long stance forward. Turn to the left and step into a left leg long stance with a left outward face block, followed by a right hand punch.

6. 오른발 돌려차고 내디디며(앞굽이 크기) 왼발 왼쪽으로 내디뎌 앞굽이 왼 얼굴바깥막고 오른 몸통지르기

7. Front kick with your right leg, landing forward in a right leg long stance with a left hand punch.

7. 오른발 앞차고 오른 앞굽이 왼 몸통지르기

# Taegeuk 6 Jang
태극 6장

8. Step back with your right foot and turn 180° to the right, making a right leg long stance and a right outward face block, followed by a left hand punch.

8. 오른쪽으로 돌아 오른 앞굽이 오른 얼굴바깥막고 왼 몸통지르기

9. Front kick with your left leg, landing forward in a left leg long stance with a right hand punch.

9. 왼발 앞차고 왼 앞굽이 오른 몸통지르기

10. Turn left toward the front and step to the side with your left foot into a parallel stance with a slow low scatter block for 5 seconds.

10. 왼쪽으로 돌아 왼발 내디뎌 나란히서기 아래헤쳐막기(5초)

# Taegeuk 6 Jang
## 태극 6장

11. Step forward into a right leg long stance with a left outward twisted knife hand face block.

11. 오른발 내디뎌 앞굽이 왼 얼굴 손날 비틀어 바깥막기

12. Left leg roundhouse kick with Kihap, landing the distance of a long stance forward. Turn 270° to the right and step into a right leg long stance with a right hand low block.

12. 왼발 돌려차고(기합) 내디디며(앞굽이 크기) 오른쪽으로 돌아 오른 앞굽이 오른 아래막기

13. Front kick with your left leg, landing back in a back stance with your right foot forward with a right outward middle block.

13. 왼발 앞차고 왼 뒷굽이 오른 바깥막기

14. Turn 180° to the left, making a left leg long stance and a left hand low block.

14. 왼쪽으로 돌아 왼 앞굽이 왼 아래막기

# Taegeuk 6 Jang
# 태극 6장

15. Front kick with your right leg, landing back in a back stance with your left foot forward with a left outward middle block.

15. 오른발 앞차고 오른 뒷굽이 왼 바깥막기

16. Turn counterclockwise toward the front, stepping back with your right leg into a back stance with your left foot forward with a left supported outward knife hand block.

16. 오른발 오른쪽으로 물러디뎌 뒷굽이 왼 손날 거들어 바깥막기

17. Step back into a back stance with your right foot forward with a right supported outward knife hand block.

17. 왼발 물러디뎌 뒷굽이 오른 손날 거들어 바깥막기

18. Step back into a left leg long stance, making a left inward palm black followed by a right hand punch.

18. 오른발 물러디뎌 앞굽이 왼 바탕손 안막고 오른 몸통지르기

# Taegeuk 6 Jang
# 태극 6장

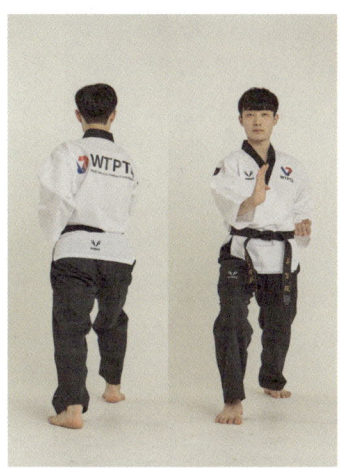

19. Step back into a right leg long stance, making a right inward palm block followed by a left hand punch.

19. 왼발 물러디뎌 앞굽이 오른 바탕손 안막고 왼 몸통지르기

Baro
바로

Important movements: Sonnal Eolgul Biteureomakgi (outward twisted knife hand face block), Eolgul Bakkanmakgi (outward face block), Arae Hecheomakgi (low scatter block), Batangson Anmakgi (inward palm block), Dollyeochagi (roundhouse kick).

# Taegeuk 7 Jang
## 태극 7장

Taegeuk 7 Jang symbolizes the Gan of Palgwe, The trigram Gan represents the mountains, signifying heaviness and firmness. In training this Poomsae, one acquires the skill and strength to train with an unshakable mind. Techniques that are introduced in this Poomsae are Sonnal Geodeureo Araemakgi (supported knife hand low block), Geodeureo Batangson Anmakgi (supported inward palm block), Bojumeok (covered fist), Gawimakgi (scissors block), Mureup Ollyeochigi (upward knee strike), Hecheomakgi (scatter block), Dujumeok Jeocheojireugi (flipped double fist punch), Utgeoreo Araemakgi (low crossing block), Deungjumeok Bakkanchigi (outward back fist strike), Pyojeokchagi (target kick), Yeopjireugi (side punch), Beomseogi (tiger stance), Juchumseogi (riding horse stance). Since there are a variety of movements, the practice of Taegeuk 7 Jang is focused on a smooth connection between each motion.(Kukkiwon, 2022).
Shape of Poomsae : 王
Number of Poom : 25

태극 7장은 팔괘의 간(艮)을 의미하며 간은 육중하고 굳건한 산을 나타낸다. 새로운 동작은 바탕손 거들어 안막기, 보주먹, 가위막기, 무릎올려치기, 헤쳐막기, 두주먹젖혀지르기, 아래엇걸어막기, 등주먹바깥치기, 표적차기, 옆지르기가 있고 서기에는 범서기와 주춤서기가 나온다. 동작이 다양하므로 연결성에 중점을 두어 수련해야 한다 (국기원, 2022).
품새선 : 王
품수 : 25

# Taegeuk 7 Jang
## 태극 7장

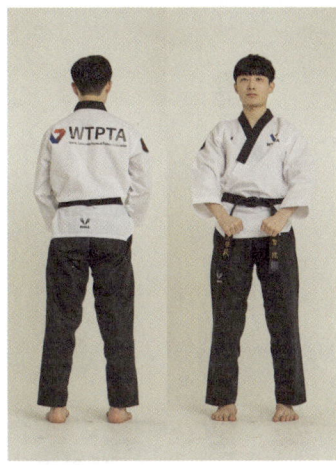

Kibon Junbiseogi

기본 준비

1. Turn to the left, making a tiger stance with your left foot forward and a right inward palm block.

1. 왼발 왼쪽으로 내디뎌 범서기 오른 바탕손 안막기

2. Front kick with your right leg, landing back in a left leg tiger stance with a left inward chest block.

2. 오른발 앞차고 왼 범서기 왼 안막기

3. Turn 180° to the right, making a right leg tiger stance and a left inward palm block.

3. 오른쪽으로 돌아 오른 범서기 왼 바탕손 안막기

4. Front kick with your left leg, landing back in a right leg tiger stance with a right inward chest block.

4. 왼발 앞차고 오른 범서기 오른 안막기

# Taegeuk 7 Jang
# 태극 7장

5. Turn left toward the front and step forward into a back stance with your left foot forward with a left supported knife hand low block.

5. 왼발 왼쪽으로 내디뎌 뒷굽이 아래 손날거들어막기

6. Step forward into a back stance with your right foot forward with a right supported knife hand low block.

6. 오른발 내디뎌 뒷굽이 아래 손날거들어막기

7-8. Turn to the left and step forward with your left foot into a left leg tiger stance with a right supported inward palm block followed by a supported right forward back fist strike to the face.

7-8. 왼발 왼쪽으로 내디뎌 범서기 오른 바탕손거들어 안막고 오른 등주먹앞치기

9-10. Turn 180° to the right, making a right leg tiger stance and a left supported inward palm block followed by a supported left forward back fist strike to the face.

9-10. 오른쪽으로 돌아 오른 범서기 왼 바탕손거들어 안막고 왼 등주먹앞치기

# Taegeuk 7 Jang
## 태극 7장

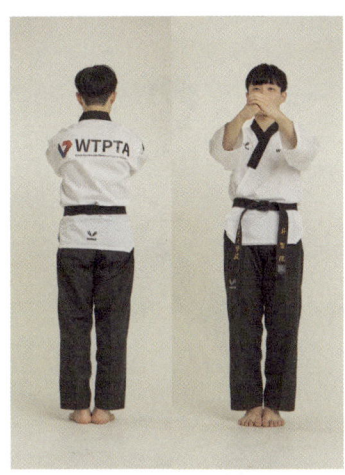

11. Turn left toward the front, moving your left foot to bring your feet together in a closed stance. Slowly raise your right covered fist for 5 seconds.

11. 왼쪽으로 돌아 모아서기 (왼발 이동) 보주먹(5초)

12. Step forward into a left leg long stance with a double scissors block (left, then right outward inner forearm block in succession).

12. 왼발 내디뎌 앞굽이 가위막기

13. Step forward into a right leg long stance with a double scissors block (right, then left outward inner forearm block in succession).

13. 오른발 내디뎌 앞굽이 가위막기

14. Turn 270° to the left and step forward with your left foot into a left leg long stance with a scatter block.

14. 왼쪽으로 돌아 왼 앞굽이 헤쳐막기

15. Knee strike with your right leg, landing the distance of one long stance forward into a cross stance with your right foot in front with a flipped double fist punch to the ribcage. Your right foot should be pointed to the right.

15. 오른 무릎올려치고 오른발 내디뎌 뒤 꼬아서기 두 주먹 젖혀지르기

# Taegeuk 7 Jang
# 태극 7장

16. Step back with your left leg into a right leg long stance with a low crossing block with your left hand on top.

16. 왼발 물러디뎌 앞굽이 아래 엇걸어막기

17. Step back with your right foot and turn 180° to the right, making a right leg long stance and a scatter block.

17. 오른쪽으로 돌아 오른 앞굽이 헤쳐막기

18. Knee strike with your left leg, landing the distance of one long stance forward into a cross stance with your left foot in front with a flipped double fist punch to the ribcage. Your left foot should be pointed to the left.

18. 왼 무릎 올려치고 왼발 내디뎌 뒤 꼬아서기 두 주먹 젖혀지르기

19. Step back with your right leg into a left leg long stance with a low crossing block with your right hand on top.

19. 오른발 물러디뎌 앞굽이 아래 엇걸어막기

# Taegeuk 7 Jang
## 태극 7장

20. Turn left toward the back and step forward with your left foot into a left leg walking stance with a left outward back fist strike to the temple.

20. 왼발 왼쪽으로 내디뎌 앞서기 왼 등주먹바깥치기

21. Crescent kick with your right leg to your left hand target, landing forward in a riding horse stance with a right elbow target strike.

21. 오른발 표적차고 주춤서기 오른 팔꿈치 표적앞치기

22. Slightly step forward with your right leg into a right leg walking stance with a right outward back fist strike to the temple.

22. 오른발 앞으로 내디뎌 앞서기 오른 등주먹바깥치기

23. Crescent kick with your left leg to your right hand target, landing forward in a riding horse stance with a left elbow target strike.

23. 왼발 표적차고 주춤서기 왼 팔꿈치 표적앞치기

# Taegeuk 7 Jang
태극 7장

24. Keeping your stance, make a left outward single knife hand block.

24. 발자세 그대로 왼 손날옆막기

25. Step forward with your right foot into a riding horse stance with a right hand punch to the side with Kihap.

25. 오른발 내디뎌 주춤서기 오른 몸통옆지르기(기합)

Baro
바로

Important movements:: Sonal Geodeureo Araemakgi (double knife hand low block), Geodeureo Batangson Anmakgi (an assisted out-to-in chest block with your palm), Geodeureo Deungjumeok Apchigi (back fist), Bojumeok (covered fist), Gawimakgi (scissors block), Mureupchigi (knee strike), Hecheomakgi (double middle block), Dujumeok Jeocheojireugi (double uppercut to the ribcage), Utgeoreo Araemakgi (cross low block), Deungjumeok Bakkanchigi (forward backfist), Pyojeokchagi (crescent kick to hand target), Yeopjireugi (Side punch))
Important Stances: Beomseogi (tiger stance), Juchumseogi (riding horse stance)

# Taegeuk 8 Jang
## 태극 8장

Taegeuk 8 Jang symbolizes the Gon of Palgwe. The trigram Gon is associated with Yin or "earth", as well as the root and settlement, the beginning and the end. This is the last of the 8 Taegeuk Poomsaes. Techniques that are introduced in this Poomsae Dubaldangseongchagi (jumping double front kick), Geodeureo Bakkanmakgi (supported outward block), Oesanteulmakgi (single mountain block), Danggyeojireugi (pulling uppercut), Geodeureo Araemakgi (supported low block), Ttwieoapchagi (jumping front kick), Palggumchi Dollyeochigi (elbow turning strike). (Kukkiwon, 2022).
Shape of Poomsae: 王
Number of Poom: 27

태극 8장은 팔괘의 곤(坤)을 의미하며 곤은 음(陰)의 기운인 땅을 나타낸다. 유급자의 마지막 품새로서 연성이 끝나면 1장에서 8장까지 총연습 기간을 거쳐 국기원 승품(단)심사에 나갈 수 있는 자격이 부여된다.
새로운 동작은 두발당성앞차기, 거들어바깥막기, 외산틀막기, 당겨턱지르기, 아래거들어막기, 뛰어앞차기, 팔꿈치 돌려치기가 있다. 수련 시 유의할 것은 발차고 뒤로 두 걸음 물러나는 보법의 정확성과 두발당성과 뛰어앞차기 동작의 차이점 습득요령이다 (국기원, 2022).
품새선:王
품수:27

# Taegeuk 8 Jang
# 태극 8장

Kibon Junbiseogi

기본 준비

1. Step forward into a back stance with your left foot forward with a supported left outward middle block

1. 왼발 앞으로 내디뎌
   뒷굽이 거들어바깥막기

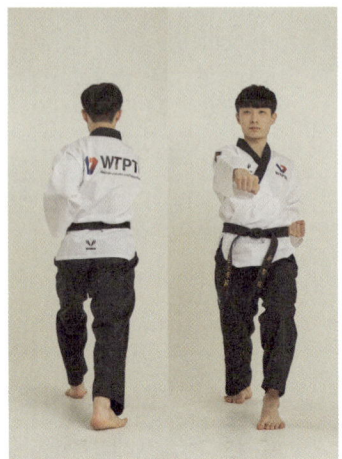

2. Slightly step forward with your left foot into a left leg long stance with a right hand punch.

2. 왼발 내디뎌 앞굽이
   오른 몸통지르기

3. Double front kick with Kihap, landing forward into a left leg long stance with a left inward chest block, followed by a double punch (right, then left hand punch in succession).

3. 두발당성 앞차고(기합) 왼 앞굽이
   왼 안막고 두 번 지르기(오른-왼)

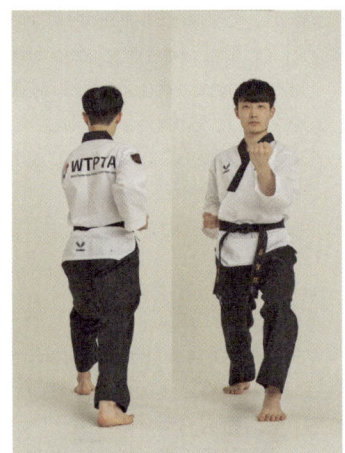

# Taegeuk 8 Jang
## 태극 8장

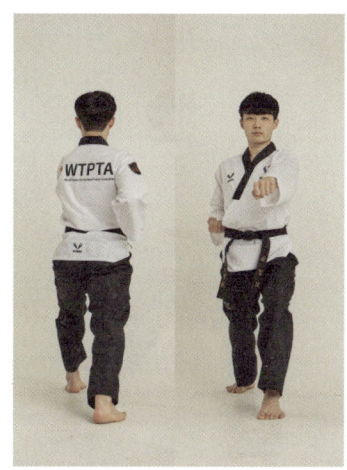

4. Step forward into a right leg long stance with a right hand punch.

4. 오른발 내디뎌 앞굽이 오른 몸통지르기

5. Turn 270° to the left and step forward with your left foot into a long right leg parallel stance with a single mountain block (right hand high inner forearm outside block, left hand low block).

5. 왼쪽으로 돌아 오른 앞굽이 외산틀막기(모앞굽이 형태로)

6. While facing the same direction, turn your body and slightly step with your left foot into a left leg long stance. Slowly pull your left hand to your right shoulder and make a supported pulling punch with your right hand for 8 seconds.

6. 왼발 옮겨 디뎌 앞굽이 오른 턱당겨지르기(8초)

7. Turn 180° to the right and step over your right foot with your left in a cross stance, then step to the right with your right foot, landing in a long left leg parallel stance with a single mountain block (left hand inner forearm outside block, right hand low block).

7. 꼬아서기 형태로 왼발 옮겨 디딘 후 왼 앞굽이 외산틀막기(모앞굽이 형태)

# Taegeuk 8 Jang
## 태극 8장

8. Facing the same direction, turn your body and slightly step with your right foot into a right leg long stance. Slowly pull your right hand to your left shoulder and make an a supported pulling punch for 8 seconds.

8. 오른발 옮겨 디뎌 앞굽이 왼 턱당겨지르기(8초)

9. Turn left to face the front and step back with your right foot into a back stance with your left foot forward with a left supported knife hand block.

9. 오른쪽으로 돌아 오른발 물러디뎌 뒷굽이 손날거들어바깥막기

10. Slightly step forward with your left foot into a left leg long stance with a right hand punch.

10. 왼발 내디뎌 앞굽이 오른 몸통지르기

11. Front kick with your right leg, landing back in a left leg walking stance. Step back into a right leg walking stance, then pull your right foot back into a right leg tiger stance with a right inward palm block.

11. 오른발 앞차고 오른발, 왼발 물러디뎌 오른 범서기(앞발을 끌어당긴다) 오른 바탕손 안막기

# Taegeuk 8 Jang
## 태극 8장

12. Turn to the left into a left leg tiger stance with a left supported knife hand block.

12. 왼발 왼쪽으로 내디뎌 범서기 왼 손날거들어바깥막기

13. Front kick with your left leg, landing forward in a left leg long stance with a right hand punch.

13. 왼발 앞차고 왼 앞굽이 오른 몸통지르기

14. Pull your left foot back into a left leg tiger stance with a left inward palm block.

14. 왼발 끌어당겨 왼 범서기 왼 바탕손안막기

15. Turn your body 180° to the right, making a right leg tiger stance and a right hand supported knife hand block.

15. 오른쪽으로 돌아 오른 범서기 오른 손날거들어바깥막기

16. Front kick with your right leg, landing forward in a right leg long stance with a left hand punch.

16. 오른발 앞차고 오른 앞굽이 왼 몸통지르기

# Taegeuk 8 Jang
# 태극 8장

17. Pull your right foot back into a right leg tiger stance with a right inward palm block.

17. 오른발 끌어당겨 오른 범서기 오른 바탕손 안막기

18. Turn right toward the back and step forward with your right foot into a back stance with your right foot forward with supported right hand low block.

18. 오른발 오른쪽으로 내디뎌 뒷굽이 아래거들어막기

19. Front kick with your left leg to the face, then jump with a right leg front kick with Kihap, landing forward into a right leg long stance with a right hand inward chest block, followed by a double punch (left, then right hand punch in succession).

19. 왼 앞차고 오른 뛰어 앞차고(기합) 오른 앞굽이 오른 안막고 두번지르기(왼-오른)

# Taegeuk 8 Jang
# 태극 8장

20. Turn 270° to the left and step forward into a back stance with your left foot forward with a left outward single knife hand block.
20. 왼쪽으로 돌아 오른 뒷굽이 왼 손날바깥막기

21. Slightly step forward with your left foot into a left leg long stance with a right hand elbow strike to the chin.
21. 왼발 내디뎌 앞굽이 오른 얼굴팔꿈치돌려치기

22. Keeping your stance, with your right hand, back fist forward strike.
22. 발자세 그대로 오른 등주먹앞치기

23. Keeping your stance, punch with your left hand.
23. 발자세 그대로 왼 몸통지르기

# Taegeuk 8 Jang
## 태극 8장

24. Turn 180° to the right, making a back stance with your right foot forward with a right outward single knife hand block.

24. 오른발 돌아디뎌 왼 뒷굽이 오른 손날 바깥막기

25. Slightly step forward with your right foot into a right leg long stance with a left hand elbow strike to the chin.

25. 오른발 내디뎌 앞굽이 왼 얼굴팔꿈치돌려치기

26. Keeping your stance, back fist forward strike to the face with your left hand.

26. 발자세 그대로 왼 등주먹앞치기

27. Keeping your stance, punch with your right hand.

27. 발자세 그대로 오른 몸통지르기

Baro
바로

Important movements: Dubaldangseongchagi (double front kick), Geodeureo Bakkanmakgi (supported outward block), Oesanteulmakgi (single mountain block), Danggyeojireugi (pulling uppercut), Geodeureo Araemakgi (supported low block), Ttwieoapchagi (jumping front kick)

# Koryo
## 고려

The Koryo Poomsae was created to symbolize Seonbae, which means a learned man. Seonbae is characterized by a strong and righteous martial artist spirit inherited through the ages of Koguryeo (an ancient Korean dynasty from 37 B.C.E–668 C.E), Balhae (an ancient Korean dynasty from 698–926 C.E) and down to Koryo (an ancient Korean dynasty from 935–1392 C.E).

Techniques that are introduced in this Poomsae are Geodeupyeopchagi (double side kick), Sonnal Bakkanchigi (knife hand outward neck strike), Sonnal Araemakgi (knife hand low block), Kaljebi (arc hand strike), Batangson Nulleomakgi (palm pressing block), Anpalmok Hecheomakgi (inner wrist scatter block), Pyojeokjireugi (target punch), Pyeonsonkeut Jeocheojjireugi (palm-up thrust), Palggumchi Yeopchigi (supported elbow side strike), Mejumeok Pyojeokaraechigi (hammer fist target strike hitting underneath).

The ready stance position, Tongmilgi, requires mental concentration by positioning the hand in between the upper abdomen and the lower abdomen where Sin (meaning divine) and Jeong (meaning spirit) converge. (Kukkiwon, 2022).

The shape of Poomsae represents the '士' which means Seonbae (Seonbi).

Number of Poom : 30

Ready stance(Tongmilgi): Step to the left with your left foot into a parallel stance one foot apart. At the same time, inhale with your palms facing each other and your fingertips pointed down, your solar plexus from the lower part of your abdomen. Exhale and push your hands away from your face.

고려는 선배를 의미하며 선배는 강력한 상무정신과 곧은 선비정신을 나타내고 고구려-발해-고려로 이어지는 선배(선비)의 얼을 바탕으로 하여 품새로 엮어졌다.

새로운 동작은 거듭차기, 손날바깥치기, 손날아래막기, 아금손앞치기, 무릎눌러꺾기, 안팔목헤쳐막기, 표적옆지르기, 아래젖혀찌르기, 바탕손눌러막기, 팔꿈치거들어옆치기, 메주먹 표적 안치기 등으로 태극품새와는 달리 유단자 품새다운 기술이 많이 나온다. 준비서기는 통밀기 이며 손의 위치가 상단전과 중단전사이로 신(神)과 정(精)이 합쳐지는 지점이므로 정신통일을 중요하게 생각하는 서기이다(국기원, 2022).

품새선: '士'자로 고려품새의 의미인 선배(선비)의 표상이다.

품수:30품

# Koryo
# 고려

Tongmilgi Junbiseogi

통밀기 준비

1. Turn to the left, making a back stance with your left foot forward and a left supported knife hand block.

1. 왼발 왼쪽으로 내디뎌 뒷굽이 손날거들어바깥막기

2. Double side kick with your right leg, landing forward into a right leg long stance with a right outer knife hand strike to the neck.

2. 오른발 거듭옆차고 오른 앞굽이 오른 손날바깥치기(목 높이)

3. Keeping your stance, punch with your left hand.

3. 발자세 그대로 몸통지르기

# Koryo
## 고려

4. Slightly pull your right foot back into a back stance with your right foot forward with a right inward chest block.

4. 오른발 당겨 뒷굽이 오른 안막기

5. Step back with your right foot and turn 180° to the right, making a back stance with your right foot forward and a right supported knife hand block.

5. 오른쪽으로 돌아 왼 뒷굽이 오른 손날거들어바깥막기

6. Double side kick with your left leg, landing forward into a left leg long stance with a left outer knife hand strike to the neck.

6. 왼발 거듭옆차고 왼 앞굽이 왼 손날바깥치고 (목 높이)

7. Keeping your stance, punch with your right hand.

7. 발자세 그대로 오른 몸통지르기

# Koryo
고려

8. Slightly pull your left foot back into a back stance with your left foot forward with a left inward chest block.

8. 왼발 당겨 뒷굽이 왼 안막기

9. Turn left toward the front and step forward into a left leg long stance with a left open hand low block, followed by a right arc hand strike.

9. 왼발 왼쪽으로 내디뎌 앞굽이 왼 손날 아래막고 오른 아금손앞치기(목 높이)

10. Front kick with your right leg, landing forward into a right leg long stance with a right open hand low block, followed by a left arc hand strike.

10. 오른발 앞차고 오른 앞굽이 오른 손날아래막고 왼 아금손앞치기 (목 높이)

# Koryo
## 고려

11. Front kick with your left leg, landing forward into a left leg long stance with a left open hand low block, followed by a right arc hand strike with Kihap.

11. 왼발 앞차고 왼 앞굽이 왼 손날 아래막고 오른 아금손앞치기 (목 높이, 기합)

12. Front kick with your right leg, landing forward into a right leg long stance with a left arc hand knee strike.

12. 오른발 앞차고 오른 앞굽이 무릎눌러꺾기

13. Step forward with your left foot and turn to face the back in a right leg long stance with an inner wrist scatter block.

13. 오른쪽으로 돌아 오른 앞굽이 안팔목헤쳐막기

# Koryo
고려

14. Front kick with your left leg, landing forward into a left leg long stance with a right arc hand knee strike.

14. 왼발 앞차고 왼 앞굽이 무릎눌러꺾기

15. Pull your left foot back into a left leg walking stance with an inner wrist scatter block.

15. 왼발 당겨 앞서기 안팔목헤쳐막기

16. Turn 270° to the right and step to the side with your right foot to make a riding horse stance with a left outward single knife hand block, followed by a right hand punch to your left hand target.

16. 오른쪽으로 돌아디뎌 주춤서기 왼 손날옆막고 표적옆지르기

17. Step with your right foot over your left foot into a cross stance, then sidekick with your left foot while pulling your hands into a right small hinge. Land into a right leg long stance with a left hand palm-up thrust facing the opposite direction from your side kick.

17. 오른 앞꼬아서기로 옮겨디뎌 왼발 옆차기와 동시에 작은돌쩌귀 하고 오른 앞굽이 왼 아래젖혀찌르기

# Koryo
고려

18. Pull your right leg back into a right leg walking stance with a right hand low block.
18. 오른발 당겨 앞서기 오른 아래막기

19. Step forward with your left leg into a left leg walking stance with a left palm hand pressing block.
19. 왼발 내디뎌 앞서기 왼 바탕손눌러막기

20. Step forward with your right leg into a riding horse stance with a right supported elbow strike to the side, followed by a right outward knife hand block and left hand target punch.
20. 오른발 내디뎌 주춤서기 오른 팔꿈치거들어 옆치고 오른 손날옆막고 표적옆지르기

# Koryo
## 고려

21. Step with your left foot over your right foot into a cross stance, then sidekick with your right foot while pulling your hands into a left small hinge. Land into a left leg long stance with a right hand palm-up thrust facing the opposite direction from your side kick.

21. 왼발 앞꼬아서기로 옮겨디뎌 오른발 옆차기와 동시에 작은돌쩌귀 하고 왼 앞굽이 아래젖혀찌르기

22. Pull your left leg back into a left leg walking stance with a left hand low block.

22. 왼발 당겨 앞서기 왼 아래막기

23. Step forward with your right leg into a right leg walking stance with a right hand down block.

23. 오른발 내디뎌 앞서기 오른 바탕손눌러막기

# Koryo
## 고려

24. Step forward with your left foot into a riding horse stance with a left supported elbow strike to the sied.
24. 왼발 내디뎌 주춤서기 왼 팔꿈치거 들어옆치기

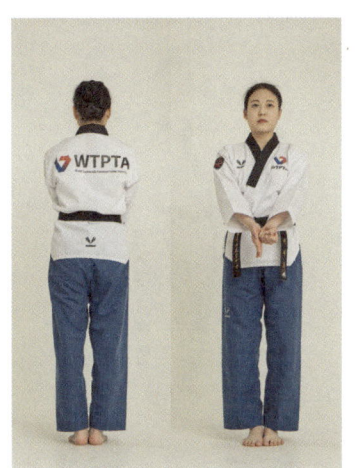

25. Move your right foot in to bring your feet together into a closed stance. Starting with both hands open above your head, slowly lower your hands and make a left hand hammer fist to your right hand target for 8 seconds. Start making a closed fist when your hands reach shoulder height.
25. 모아서기(오른발 이동, 이때 두 손이 머리위에 위치) 왼 아래 메주먹 표적 안치기(두 손이 어깨선에 왔을 때 왼주먹을 말아쥐기시작)(8초)

26. Turn left to face the back and step forward to a left leg long stance with a left knife hand outward neck strike, followed by a left open hand low block.
26. 왼쪽으로 돌아 왼 앞굽이 왼 손날 바깥치고(목 높이) 왼 아래손날막기

27. Step forward into a right leg long stance with a right inward hand strike to the neck, followed by a right open hand low block.
27. 오른발 내디뎌 앞굽이 오른 손날안치고(목 높이) 오른 아래손날막기

# Koryo
## 고려

28. Step forward into a left leg long stance with a left inward knife hand neck strike, followed by a left open hand low block.

28. 왼발 내디뎌 앞굽이 왼 손날안치고 (목 높이) 왼 아래손날막기

29. Step forward into a right leg long stance with a right arc hand strike with Kihap.

29. 오른발 내디뎌 앞굽이 오른 아금손앞치기 (목 높이, 기합)

바로

Important movements: Geodeupyeopchagi (Double side kick), Sonnal Bakkanchigi (knife hand outward neck strike), Ageumson Apchigi (arc hand strike), Ageumson Mureupkuk-ki (arc hand knee strike), Anpalmok Hecheomakgi (inner wrist scatter bolck), Jageundoljjeogwi (small hinge), Pyeonsonkeut Jeocheojjireugi (palm-up thrust), Batangson Nulleomakgi (palm hand pressing block), Palggumchi Yeopchigi (supported elbow strike to side), Mejumeok Pyojeokaraechigi (hammer fist target strike hitting underneath)

# Keumgang
## 금강

Keumgang symbolizes hardness and ponderosity. This Poomsae was named after Mount Keumgang on the Korean peninsula, which is regarded as the center of national spirit. Mount Keumgang was named by Buddha, who represents the mightiest warrior.
Key techniques that are used in the Poomsae are Batangson Apchigi (palm hand forward strike), Sonnal Anmakgi (inward knife hand block), Keumgangmakgi (diamond block), Santeulmakgi (mountain block), Keundoljjeogwi (large hinge), and Hakdariseogi (crane stance) (Kukkiwon, 2022).
Shape of Poomsae : '山' (This Poomsae is in the shape of the chinese character for mountain. The chinese symbol also means grandeur and stability. When practicing this Poomsae, you must train slowly with powerful movements, and train your center of balance.)
Number of Poom : 27


금강은 더할 수 없이 강함과 무거움을 의미하며 강함과 무거움은 한반도의 정기가 모인 영산인 금강산과 부처의 호법으로 두 신장(神將)이며 무술이 가장 세다는 금강역사 가운데 더욱 강맹하고 파괴되지 않으며, 남성을 상징하는 금강을 나타내고 이 두 가지 요소가 한데 어울려 품새가 되었다.
새로운 동작은 얼굴바탕손앞치기, 손날안막기, 금강막기, 산틀막기, 큰돌쩌귀 등이고 서기로는 학다리서기가 있다(국기원, 2022).
품새선: '山'자로 되어 있으며 뜻은 웅장함과 안정성이므로 품새의 수련 시 동작은 힘 있고 강하게 중심을 안정시켜 천천히 행하여 힘을 길러야 하며 유단자의 위용이 나타나야 한다.
품수:27품

# Keumgang
# 금강

Kibon Junbiseogi

기본 준비

1. Step forward into a left leg long stance with an inner wrist scatter block.

1. 왼발 앞으로 내디뎌 앞굽이 안팔목헤쳐막기

2. Step forward into a right leg long stance and right palm hand forward strike.

2. 오른발 내디뎌 앞굽이 오른 얼굴바탕손앞치기

3. Step forwards into a left leg long stance and left palm hand forward strike to the jaw.

3. 왼발 내디뎌 앞굽이 왼 얼굴바탕손앞치기

4. Step forwards into a right leg long stance and right palm hand forward strike to the jaw.

4. 오른발 내디뎌 앞굽이 오른발 내디뎌 앞굽이 오른 얼굴바탕손앞치기

5. Step back with your right leg into a back stance with your left foot forward and a left inward knife hand chest block.

5. 오른발 물러디뎌 뒷굽이 왼 손날안막기

# Keumgang
# 금강

6. Step back with your left leg into a back stance and your right foot forward and a right inward knife hand chest block.

6. 왼발 물러디뎌 뒷굽이 오른 손날안막기

7. Step back with your right leg into a back stance with your left foot forward and a left inward knife hand chest block.

7. 오른발 물러디뎌 뒷굽이 왼 손날안막기

8. Lift your left foot up into a crane stance with a slow diamond block for 8 seconds (left hand low block, right hand high block).

8. 오른 학다리서기 금강막기(8초)

9. Step to the left with your left foot, making a riding horse stance with a right large hinge.

9. 왼발 옆디뎌 주춤서기 오른 큰돌쩌귀

10. Step with your right foot in front of your left foot to spin around, landing in a riding horse stance and a right large hinge.

10. 오른발 옮겨디뎌 돌아 주춤서기 오른 큰돌쩌귀

# Keumgang
# 금강

11. Raise your right foot to turn 90° left, landing with a stomp in a riding horse stance with a mountain block with Kihap, looking toward the front.

11. 오른발 짓찧으며 주춤서기 산틀막기 (시선은 오른손, 기합)

12. Step forward with your left foot into a riding horse stance with an inner wrist scatter block.

12. 오른쪽으로 돌아 왼발 내디뎌 주춤서기 안팔목헤쳐막기

13. Slide your left foot in to make a parallel stance, slowly making a low scatter block for 5 seconds.

13. 왼발 당겨 나란히서기 아래헤쳐막기(5초)

14. Turn right towards the back and raise your left foot, stepping forward with your left foot and landing with a stomp in a riding horse stance with a mountain block, looking toward the back.

14. 오른쪽으로 돌아 왼발 짓찧으며 주춤서기 산틀막기(시선은 왼손)

15. Turn right to face the front, lifting your right foot to make a crane stance with a slow diamond block for 8 seconds (right hand low block, left hand high block).

15. 오른쪽으로 돌아 왼 학다리서기 금강막기(8초)

16. Step to the right with your right foot, making a riding horse stance with a large left hinge.

16. 오른발 옆디뎌 주춤서기 왼 큰돌쩌귀

# Keumgang
## 금강

17. Step with your left foot in front of your right foot to spin around, landing in a riding horse stance with a large left hinge.

17. 왼발 옮겨디뎌 돌아 주춤서기 왼 큰돌쩌귀

18. Lift your right leg up into a crane stance with a slow diamond block for 8 seconds (right hand low block, left hand high block).

18. 왼 학다리서기 금강막기(8초)

19. Step to the right with your right foot, making a riding horse stance with a large left hinge.

19. 오른발 옆디뎌 주춤서기 왼 큰돌쩌귀

20. Step with your left foot in front of your right foot to spin around, landing in a riding horse stance with a large left hinge.

20. 왼발 옮겨디디며 돌아 주춤서기 왼 큰돌쩌귀

# Keumgang
# 금강

21. Raise your left foot to turn 90° right, landing with a stomp in a riding horse stance with a mountain block with Kihap, looking toward the front.

21. 왼발 짓찧으며 주춤서기 산틀막기 (시선은 왼손, 기합)

22. Step forward with your right foot into a riding horse stance with an inner wrist scatter block.

22. 왼쪽으로 돌아 오른발 내디뎌 주춤서기 안팔목헤쳐막기

23. Slide your right foot in to make a parallel stance, slowly making a low scatter block for 5 seconds.

23. 오른발 당겨 나란히서기 아래헤쳐막기(5초)

24. Turn left towards the back and raise your right foot, stepping forward with your right foot and landing with a stomp in a riding horse stance with a mountain block, looking toward the back.

24. 오른쪽으로 돌아 오른발 짓찧으며 주춤서기 산틀막기(시선은 오른손)

25. Turn left to face the front, lifting your left foot to make a crane stance with a slow diamond block for 8 seconds (left hand low block, right hand high block).

25. 왼쪽으로 돌아 오른 학다리서기 금강막기(8초)

26. Step to the left with your left foot, making a riding horse stance with a right large hinge.

26. 왼발 옆디뎌 주춤서기 오른 큰돌쩌귀

# Keumgang
## 금강

27. Step with your right foot in front of your left foot to spin around, landing in a riding horse stance and a right large hinge.

27. 오른발 옮겨디뎌 돌아 주춤서기 오른 큰돌쩌귀

Baro
바로

Important movements: Batangson Apchigi (palm hand forward strike), Sonnal Anmakgi (inward knife hand chest block), Geumgangmakgi (diamond block), Keundoljjeogwi (large hinge), Dola Keundoljjeogwi (turning large hinge), Santeul-makgi (mountain block), Jitjitgi (stomp).
Critical Stance: Hakdariseogi(crane stance)

# Taebaek
# 태백

Taebaek is the name of a mountain with the meaning of "bright mountain," where the founder of the Korean nation Dangun reigned over the country. The bright mountain symbolizes the sacredness of the soul and Dangun's thought of Hongik Ingan, the humanitarian ideal.
There are numerous sites claiming to be the Taebaek mountain where Dangun reigned, Mount Paekdu, known as the foundation of Korean people, was the origin in naming the Taebaek Poomsae.
Techniques that are introduced in this Poomsae are Sonnal Araehecheomakgi (low knife hand scatter block), sonnal Eopeojapgi (knife hand palm-down grasp), Teureoppaegi (turning pull away), Geumgang Bakkan-makgi (outward inner wrist diamond block). (Kukkiwon, 2022).
Shape of Poomsae: '工' (The shape of this Poomsae resembling a human connecting the open sky and earth. The movements in this Poomsae consist mainly of blocks and strikes to the body.)
Number of Poom : 26

태백은 한민족의 고대국가인 단군조선이 개국한 아사달(아씨땅)의 성산인 붉메(밝은산)를 의미하며 밝은산은 얼과 전통의 근원, 신선함을 그리고 홍익인간의 사상을 나타낸다. 태백은 수없이 다른 위치와 말로 나타나 있지만 그 가운데 대표적인 것이 민족의 태반(胎盤)이고 상징인 백두산이며 단군의 높은 이상을 바탕으로 품새가 생겨났다.
새로운 동작은 아래손날헤쳐막기, 안팔목금강바깥막기, 손목밑으로빼기 이다(국기원, 2022).
품새선: '工' 자로 열린 하늘과 땅 사이를 사람이 올바로 이어주는 개천(開天)과 개국(開國)을 뜻하며 품새의 동작은 몸통의 막기와 치기로 주로 구성되어 하늘과 땅사이에 바로 선 사람을 나타냈다.
품수:26품

# Taebaek
## 태백

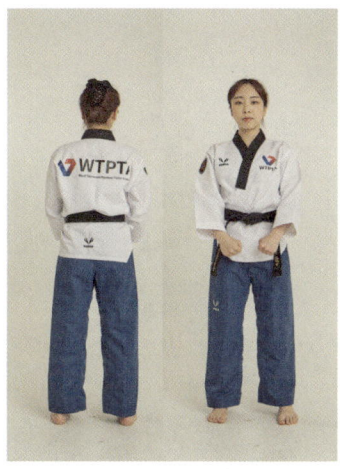

Kibon Junbiseogi

기본 준비

1. Turn to the left, making a left leg tiger stance and a low knife hand scatter bolck.

1. 왼발 왼쪽으로 내디뎌 범서기 아래손날헤쳐막기

2. Front kick with your right leg, landing forward in a right leg long stance with a double punch (right, then left hand punch in succession).

2. 오른발 앞차고 오른 앞굽이 두번지르기(오른-왼)

3. Step back with your right foot and turn 180° to the right, making a right leg tiger stance and a low knife hand scatter bolck.

3. 오른쪽으로 돌아 오른 범서기 아래손날헤쳐막기

# Taebaek
## 태백

4. Front kick with your left leg, landing forward in a left leg long stance with a double punch (left, then right hand punch in succession).

4. 왼발 앞차고 왼 앞굽이 두번지르기 (왼-오른)

5. Turn left towards the front and step forward with your left foot into a left leg long stance with a swallow shaped strike (left hand open hand high block and right knife hand neck strike).

5. 왼발 왼쪽으로 내디뎌 제비품안치기 (목 높이)

6. Step forward into a right leg long stance while twisting your right hand in a circular motion, bringing your palm close to your face and then pushing your palm away from your body. Punch with your left hand.

6. 오른발 내디디며 오른손 안에서 밖으로 젖혀틀어 상대팔목 잡아당기며 오른 앞굽이 왼 몸통지르기

# Taebaek
## 태백

7. Step forward into a left leg long stance while twisting your left hand in a circular motion, bringing your palm close to your face and then pushing your palm away from your body. Punch with your right hand.

7. 왼발 내디디며 왼손 안에서 밖으로 젖혀틀어 상대팔목 잡아당기며 왼 앞굽이 오른 몸통지르기

8. Step forward with your right leg into a right leg long stance while twisting your right hand in a circular motion, bringing your palm close to your face and then pushing your palm away from your body. Punch with your left hand with Kihap.

8. 오른발 내디디며 오른손 안에서 밖으로 젖혀틀어 상대팔목 잡아당기며오른 앞굽이 왼 몸통지르기(기합)

9. Turn to the left and step forward with your left foot into a back stance with your left foot forward with an outward inner wrist diamond block (left outward inner wrist block, right hand high block).

9. 왼쪽으로 돌아 오른 뒷굽이 안팔목금강바깥막기

10. Keeping your stance, pull your left hand up to your shoulder to make a chin pulling punch motion with your right hand.

10. 발자세 그대로 오른 턱당겨지르기

# Taebaek
태백

11. Keeping your stance, punch with your left hand.

11. 발자세 그대로 왼 지르기

12. Lift your left foot up into a crane stance with a small right hinge.

12. 오른 학다리서기 오른 작은돌쩌귀

13. Side kick with your left leg with a left hammer fist strike to the side, landing forward in a left leg long stance with right elbow target strike.

13. 왼발 옆차기와 동시에 왼 메주먹바깥치고 왼 앞굽이 오른 팔꿈치표적 앞치기

14. Looking to the right, step with your left foot to put your feet together, then step out with your right foot to make a back stance with your right leg forward with an outward inner wrist diamond block (right outward inner wrist block, left hand high block).

14. 오른쪽으로 돌아 왼발 옮겨디뎌 모아선 후 오른발 내디뎌 뒷굽이 안팔목금강바깥막기

# Taebaek
## 태백

15. Keeping your stance, pull your right hand up to your shoulder to make a chin pulling punch motion with your left hand.

15. 발자세 그대로 왼 당겨턱지르기

16. Keeping your stance, punch with your right hand.

16. 발자세 그대로 오른 지르기

17. Lift your right foot into a crane stance with a small left hinge.

17. 왼 학다리서기 왼 작은돌쩌귀

18. Side kick with your right leg with a right hammer fist strike to the side, landing forward in a right leg long stance with left elbow target strike to your right hand target.

18. 오른발 옆차기와 동시에 오른 메주먹바깥치고 오른 앞굽이 왼 팔꿈치표적앞치기

19. Step with your right foot to put your feet together and turn left toward the back. Step forward with your left foot into a back stance with your left foot forward with a left supported outward knife hand block.

19. 오른발 당겨 모아선 후 왼발 왼쪽으로 내디뎌 뒷굽이 손날거들어바깥막기

# Taebaek
## 태백

20. Step forward into a right leg long stance with a right supported upright thrust.

20. 오른발 내디뎌 앞굽이 오른 거들어세워찌르기

21. Step to the side with your left foot to change your stance into a left leg long stance with the right hand which was grasped pulling down.(Keep looking toward the back.) Step forward into a back stance with your left foot forward with a left back fist outward face strike.

21. 왼쪽으로 돌아 왼발 옮겨디뎌 앞굽이(시선은 오른쪽 유지) 오른 잡힌손목밑으로 빼며 왼쪽으로 돌아 오른 뒷굽이 왼 등주먹바깥치기(얼굴 높이)

22. Step forward into a right leg long stance with a right hand punch with Kihap.

22. 오른발 내디뎌 앞굽이 오른 몸통지르기(기합)

23. Turn 270° to the left and step with your left foot into a left leg long stance with a scissors block (left hand low block, right hand outward inner wrist block).

23. 왼쪽으로 돌아 왼 앞굽이 가위막기

# Taebaek
## 태백

24. Front kick with your right leg, landing forward in a right leg long stance with a double punch (right, then left hand punch in succession).
24. 오른발 앞차고 오른 앞굽이 두번지르기(오른-왼)

25. Step back with your right foot and turn 180° to the right, making a right leg long stance with a scissors block (right hand low block, left hand outward inner wrist block).
25. 오른쪽으로 돌아 오른 앞굽이 가위막기

26. Front kick with your left leg, landing forward in a left leg long stance with a double punch (left, then right hand punch in succession).
26. 왼발 앞차고 왼 앞굽이 두번지르기 (왼-오른)

# Taebaek
# 태백

Baro
바로

Important movements: Sonnal Araehecheomakgi (low knife hand scatter block), Keumgang Bakkanmakgi (outward inner wrist diamond block), Deungjumeok Eolgul Bakkanchigi (back fist outward face strike).

# Pyeongwon
# 평원

Pyeongwon means a large land that spreads far and wide in all directions. The large land represents the preservation of life as the birthland of living things and the foundation of life through man, the lord of all things. This Poomsae originated and was practiced on the basis of peace and combat.

Techniques that are introduced in this Poomsae are Palggumchi Ollyeochigi (elbow upward strike), Geodeureo Eolgul Yeopmakgi (supported side inner wrist face block), Danggyeo deungjumeok Apchigi (pulling back fist forward strIke), Meongyechigi (yoke-shaped strike), Hecheo Santeulmakgi (scattered mountain block) (Kukkiwon, 2022).

Shape of Poomsae: '一' (The shape of this Poomsae signifies a change with the original nature of the plain)
Number of Poom : 21
Ready stance (Oen Gyeopson): Keeping your feet together in a closed stance, place your left hand on the back of your right hand, so that both hands overlap and your palms face away from your body. Your hands should be in the shape of an X. Inhale and slowly raise your hands to your solar plexus, exhale, and slowly lower your hands to the lower part of the abdomen with your palms facing towards your body.

평원은 아득한 사방으로 넓게 펼쳐진 큰 땅을 의미하며 큰 땅은 생물의 모체로서 생명의 보존과 만물의 영장인 사람으로 인한 삶의 터전을 나타내고 본디(本)와 쓰임(用)에 따른 평화와 투쟁을 바탕으로 품새가 이루어졌다. 새로운 동작은 팔꿈치올려치기, 얼굴안팔목거들어옆막기, 등주먹거들어앞치기, 멍에치기, 헤쳐 산틀막기 등이다. 준비서기인 모아서기 왼겹손은 땅이 삶의 시작과 근본인 것 같이 인체의 힘의 근원인 하단전의 기운을 모으고 얻어서 행동하기 위한 서기이다(국기원, 2022).

품새선: '一' 평원의 본디와 바낌을 뜻한다.
품수:21품

# Pyeongwon
평원

Kyopson Junbiseogi

겹손 준비

1. Step to the left with your left foot to make a parallel stance with a slow low scatter block.

1. 왼발 옆디뎌 나란히서기 아래손날헤쳐막기(겹손에서 바로)

2. Keeping your stance, raise your open hands to make a slow Tong-milgi for 8 seconds.

2. 발자세 그대로 통밀기(8초)

3. Turn to the right, making a back stance with your right foot forward and a right knife hand low hand.

3. 오른발 오른쪽으로 내디뎌 왼 뒷굽이 아래손날막기

4. Turn to the left, making a back stance with your left foot forward and a left outward single knife hand middle block.

4. 왼쪽으로 돌아 오른 뒷굽이 손날바깥막기

5. Slightly step forward with your left foot into a left leg long stance with a right upward elbow strike.

5. 왼발 내디뎌 앞굽이 오른 팔꿈치올려치기(턱 높이)

# Pyeongwon
## 평원

6. Front kick with your right leg, followed by a left leg turning side kick, landing in a back stance with a right supported knife hand middle block.

6. 오른발 앞차고 왼발 뒤돌아 옆차고 왼 뒷굽이 오른 손날거들어바깥막기

7. Keeping your stance, swing your arms in a circular motion above your head to make a right supported knife hand low block.

7. 발자세 그대로 아래손날거들어막기

8. Slightly step with your right foot into a riding horse stance with a right supported side inner wrist face block.

8. 오른발 옮겨디뎌 주춤서기 오른 얼굴안팔목거들어옆막기

9. Raise your right foot up, then stomp on the ground in a riding horse stance with two pulling back fist forward strikes (right, then left in succession) with Kihap.

9. 오른발 짓찧으며 주춤서기 오른 얼굴등주먹거들어앞치기(기합) 왼 얼굴등주먹거들어앞치기

# Pyeongwon
평원

10. Step with your left foot over your right foot into a cross stance with a yoke-shaped strike, looking to the right.

10. 왼발 오른쪽으로 내디뎌 앞꼬아서기 멍에치기 (시선은 오른쪽)

11. Step to the right with your right foot into a riding horse stance with a mountain block.

11. 오른발 옆디뎌 주춤서기 헤쳐산틀막기

12. Lift your right foot up into a crane stance with a diamond block (right hand low block, left hand high block), then immediately pull your hands into a left small hinge.

12. 왼 학다리서기 금강막고 왼 작은돌쩌귀

13. Side kick with your right leg, landing forward into a right leg long stance with a left upward elbow strike.

13. 오른발 옆차고 오른 앞굽이 왼 팔꿈치올려치기(턱 높이)

# Pyeongwon
## 평원

14. Front kick with your left leg, followed by a right leg turning side kick, landing in a back stance with a left supported knife hand middle block.

14. 왼발 앞차고 오른발 뒤돌아 옆차고 오른 뒷굽이 왼 손날거들어바깥막기

15. Keeping your stance, swing your arms in a circular motion above your head to make a left supported knife hand low block.

15. 발자세 그대로 아래 손날거들어막기

16. Slightly step with your left foot into a riding horse stance with left supported side inner wrist face block.

16. 왼발 옮겨디뎌 주춤서기 왼 얼굴안팔목거들어옆막기

# Pyeongwon
# 평원

17. Raise your left foot up, then stomp on the ground in a riding horse stance with two pulling back fist forward strikes (left, then right in succession) with Kihap.

17. 왼발 짓찧으며 주춤서기
   왼 얼굴등주먹거들어앞치기(기합)
   오른 얼굴등주먹거들어앞치기

18. Step with your right foot over your left foot into a cross stance with a yoke-shaped strike looking to the left.

18. 오른발 왼쪽으로 내디뎌 앞꼬아서기 멍에치기(시선은 왼쪽)

19. Step to the left with your left leg into a riding horse stance with a mountain block.

19. 왼발 옆디뎌 주춤서기 헤쳐산틀막기

20. Lift your left foot up into a crane stance with a diamond block (left hand low block, right hand high block), then immediately pull your hands into a right small hinge.

20. 오른 학다리서기 금강막고 오른 작은돌쩌귀

# Pyeongwon
# 평원

21. Side kick with your left leg with a left hand hammer fist strike to the side, landing forward into a left leg long stance with a right elbow target strike.

21. 왼발 옆차기와 동시에
    왼 메주먹바깥치고
    왼 앞굽이 오른팔꿈치표적앞치기

Baro
바로

Important movements: Palggumchi Ollyeochigi (elbow upward strike), Geodeureo Ulgul Yeopmakgi (supported side inner wrist face block), Danggyeo Deung-jumeok Apchigi (pulling back fist forward strike), Meongyechigi (yoke shaped strike), Hecheo Santeulmakgi (scattered mountain block).

# Sipjin
# 십진

Sipjin is meant to represent longevity through its association to the number 10, which symbolizes a long life. Sipjin was inspired by Sipjangsang, which means the 10 creatures of a long life: the sun, moon, mountains, water, stones, pine trees, bullocks, turtles, deer, and cranes. These 10 creatures of long life representing human faith, hope, and love, are embodied in the Sipjin Poomsae.

Just as ten is symbolic of longevity, there are ten new motions in this Poomsae; Hwangsomakgi (bull horn block), Sonbadak Geodeureo Bakkanmakgi (palm supported inner wrist outward block), Pyeonsonkeut Eopeojjireugi (palm-down thrust), Bawimilge (rock push), Sonnaldeung Hecheomakgi (back of knife hand scatter block), Kkeureooligi, Chetdarijireugi, Pyeonson Eotgeureo Araemakge (open hand low crossing-block ) Sonnaldeung Geodeureomakgi (back of knife hand supported outward block) (Kukkiwon, 2022).

Shape of Poomsae: '十' (The shape of this Poomsae represents infinite numbers and endless combinations in the decimal system, which is the essence of the ideals of longevity)

Number of Poom：28

십진은 신선사상에서의 십장생을 의미하며 십장생은 해, 달, 산, 물, 돌, 소나무, 불로초, 거북, 사슴, 학을 일컫는 것으로 이러한 두 개의 천체와 세 개의 자연, 두 개의 식물과 세 개의 동물은 사람의 믿음과 희망과 사랑을 나타내므로 이를 상징하고 변화하는 품새이다.

새로운 동작은 십장생의 수에 따른 열 가지로 황소막기, 안팔목거들어바깥막기, 엎어찌르기, 바위밀기, 손날등헤쳐막기, 끌어올리기, 쳇다리지르기, 아래손날엇걸어막기, 손날등거들어바깥막기이다(국기원, 2022).

품새선: '十'으로 십장생의 사상근본과 십진법에 의한 무한대의 숫자 형성 그리고 무궁한 발전을 뜻한다.

품수:28품

# Sipjin
## 십진

Kibon Junbiseogi

기본 준비

1. In your parallel stance, slowly raise your fists up to your eye level for 5 seconds, then make a fast motion bull horn block.

1. 나란히 서기 황소막기(5초)

2. Turn to the left, making a back stance with your left foot forward and a plam supported left inner wrist outward block.

2. 왼발 왼쪽으로 내디뎌 뒷굽이 왼 안팔목거들어바깥막기

3. Slowly open your left fist for 5 seconds, then slightly step forward with your left leg into a left leg long stance with a right palm-down thrust followed by a double punch (left, then right hand punch in succession).

3. 주먹을 서서히 펴며 왼발 내디뎌 앞굽이 오른엎어찌르고 두번지르기(왼-오른)

# Sipjin
# 십진

4. Step forward with your right leg into a riding horse stance with a mountain block.

4. 오른발 내디뎌 주춤서기 헤쳐산틀막기

5. Step with your left foot over your right foot into a cross stance with a left hand downward block then step forward with your right foot into a riding horse stance with a right hand side punch with Kihap.

5. 앞꼬아서기 형태로 왼발 옮겨디디며 왼 눌러막기 후 오른발 내디뎌 주춤서기 오른 옆지르기(기합)

6. Step and turn 180° to the left with your right leg, making a riding horse stance and a yoke-shaped strike, looking to the right.

6. 왼쪽으로 돌아 주춤서기 (오른발 이동) 멍에치기 (시선은 오른쪽)

7. Step with your left foot to put your feet together in a closed stance, then step to the right into a back stance with your right foot forward with a plam supported right inner wrist outward block.

7. 왼발 옮겨디디며 모아서기 후 오른발 내디뎌 뒷굽이 오른 안팔목거들어바깥막기

# Sipjin
## 십진

8. Slowly open your right fist for 5 seconds, then slightly step forward with your right leg into a right leg long stance with a left palm-down thrust followed by a double punch (right, then left hand punch in succession).

8. 주먹을 서서히 펴며 오른발 내디뎌 앞굽이 왼 엎어찌르고 두번지르기(오른-왼)

9. Step forward with your left leg into a riding horse stance with a mountain block.

9. 왼발 내디뎌 주춤서기 헤쳐산틀막기

10. Step with your right foot over your left foot into a cross stance with a right hand downward block then step forward with your left foot into a riding horse stance with a left hand side punch with Kihap.

10. 앞꼬아서기 형태로 오른발 옮겨디디며 오른 눌러막기 후 왼발 내디뎌 주춤서기 왼 옆지르기(기합)

# Sipjin
# 십진

11. Step and turn 180° to the right with your left leg, making a riding horse stance and a yoke-shaped strike looking to the left.

11. 오른쪽으로 돌아 주춤서기
 (왼발 이동)
 멍에치기(시선은 왼쪽)

12. Turn right toward the back and step forward with your right foot into a back stance with your right foot forward with a palm supported right inner wrist outward block.

12. 오른쪽으로 돌아 왼 뒷굽이 오른 안팔목거들어바깥막기

13. Slowly open your right fist for 5 seconds, then slightly step with your right leg into a right leg long stance with a left palm-down thrust followed by a double punch (right, then left hand punch in succession).

13. 주먹을 서서히 펴며 오른발 내디뎌 앞굽이 왼 엎어찌르기 후 두번지르기(오른-왼)

14. Step forward with your left leg into a back stance with your left foot forward with a left supported knife hand low block.

14. 왼발 내디뎌 뒷굽이 왼 아래손날거들어막기

# Sipjin
## 십진

15. Step forward into a right leg long stance with a slow rock pushing motion for 5 seconds.

15. 오른발 내디뎌 앞굽이 바위밀기(5초)

16. Turn to the left and slightly step with your right foot into a riding horse stance with a knife hand scatter block.

16. 시선 왼쪽으로 이동하며 오른발 당겨 주춤서기 손날등헤쳐막기

17. Keeping your stance, slowly make a low knife hand scatter block for 5 seconds.

17. 발자세 그대로 아래손날헤쳐막기(5초)

18. Without moving your feet, slowly clench your fists for 3 seconds, then slowly straighten your knees for 2 seconds.

18. 발자세 그대로 두 무릎을 펴며 (큰 나란히서기) 주먹 쥐기(3초간)

19. Turn left to face the front and slightly step with your left foot into a left leg long stance with a lifting block with your left arm.

19. 왼발 왼쪽으로 옮겨디뎌 앞굽이 왼 끌어올리기

20. Keeping your stance, make a slow rock pushing motion for 5 seconds.

20. 발자세 그대로 바위밀기(5초)

# Sipjin
## 십진

21. Front kick with your right leg with your hands in a left small hinge, landing forward into a right leg long stance with a forked punch.

21. 오른발 앞차기와 동시에 왼 작은돌쩌귀하고 오른 앞굽이 쳇다리지르기

22. Front kick with your left leg with your hands in a right small hinge, landing forward into a left leg long stance with a forked punch.

22. 왼발 앞차기와 동시에 오른 작은돌쩌귀하고 왼 앞굽이 쳇다리지르기

23. Front kick with your right leg with your hands in a left small hinge, landing forward into a cross stance with a supported right back fist forward face strke with Kihap. Your right foot should be pointed to the left.

23. 오른발 앞차기와 동시에 왼 작은돌쩌귀하고 짓찧으며 뒷꼬아서기 오른 등주먹거들어앞치기(얼굴 높이, 기합)

# Sipjin
# 십진

24. Turn left toward the back and step forward into a left leg long stance with a slow rock pushing motion for 5 seconds.

24. 왼쪽으로 돌아 왼 앞굽이 바위밀기 (5초)

25. Pull your left leg back into a left leg tiger stance with an open hand crossing low block (right hand on top).

25. 왼발 당겨 범서기 아래손날엇걸어막기

26. Step forward into a back stance with your right leg forward with a back of knife hand supported outward block.

26. 오른발 내디뎌 뒷굽이 오른 손날등 거들어바깥막기

27. Step forward into a back stance with your left leg forward with a forked punch.

27. 왼발 내디뎌 뒷굽이 쳇다리지르기

28. Step forward into a back stance with your right leg forward with a forked punch.

28. 오른발 내디뎌 뒷굽이 쳇다리지르기

Baro
바로

# Sipjin
## 십진

Important movements: Hwangsomakgi (bull horn block), Sonbadak Geodeureo Bakkanmakge (palm supported inner wrist outward block), Pyeonsonkeut Eopeojjireugi (palm-down thrust), Bawimilge (rock pushing), Sonnaldeung Hecheomakgi (back of knife hand scatter block), Kkeureooligi (lifting block), Apchagi Jageundoljjeogwi (front kick with small hinge), Chetdarijireugi (forked punch), Geodeureo Deungjumeok Apchigi (a supported back fist forward face strke), Pyeonson Eotgeureo Araemakge (open hand low crossing-block), Sonaldeung Geodeureomakgi (back of knife hand supported outward block).

# Jitae
# 지태

Jitae is symbolic of a person on the ground with their two feet standing straight up, stretching toward the sky. The person standing on earth symbolizes a life and a fight in which people kick, step, and run, the fundamentals of living. The movements involved in the Jitae Poomsae have various aspects that appear in human survival and competition.
Techniques that are introduced in this Poomsae are Sonnal Eolgulmakgi (knife hand high block), Geumgang Momtongjireugi (diamond punch), Anpalmok Bakkanmakgi (outward inner wrist block), Mejumeok Yeoppyojeokchigi (hammer fist side target strike). (Kukkiwon, 2022).
Shape of Poomsae: '⊥' (The shape of this Poomsae resembles a person standing on the earth and rising from the earth toward the sky. The Jitae Poomsae represents a person who is born, who matures, and who dies on the earth.)
Number of Poom : 28

지태는 땅 위의 사람이 하늘을 향해 두 발을 딛고 선 지상인(地上人)을 의미하며 지상인은 사람이 삶의 터전인 땅 위에서 두발로 차고 밟고 뛰는 삶과 싸움을 나타내고 사람의 생존경쟁 속에서 나타나는 갖가지 양상을 동작으로 엮은 품새이다.
새로운 동작으로 손날얼굴막기, 금강앞지르기, 메주먹표적안치기 등이 나온다(국기원, 2022).
품새선: 'ㅗ'는 땅 위에서 선사람과 땅 위에서 하늘을 향해 솟구치는 사람의 모양으로 땅에서 나고 자라며 죽는 사람과 그 땅을 뜻한다.
품수:28품

# Jitae
# 지태

Kyopson Junbiseogi

기본 준비

1. Turn to the left, making a back stance with your left foot forward and a outwerd inner wrist block..

1. 왼발 왼쪽으로 내디뎌 뒷굽이 왼 안팔목바깥막기

2. Step forward into a right leg long stance with a slow right hand high block for 4 seconds.

2. 오른발 내디뎌 앞굽이 오른 얼굴막기

3. Keeping your stance, slowly punch with your left hand for 4 seconds.

3. 발자세 그대로 왼 몸통지르기(8초)

4. Step back with your right foot and turn 180° to the right, making a back stance with your right foot forward and a right outwerd inner wrist block.

4. 오른쪽으로 돌아 왼 뒷굽이 오른 안팔목바깥막기

5. Step forward into a left leg long stance with a slow left hand high block for 4 seconds.

5. 왼발 내디뎌 앞굽이 왼 얼굴막기

# Jitae
# 지태

6. Keeping your stance, slowly punch with your right hand for 4 seconds.

6. 발자세 그대로 오른 몸통지르기(8초)

7. Turn left toward the front and step forward into a left leg long stance with a left hand low block.

7. 왼발 왼쪽으로 내디뎌 앞굽이 왼 아래막기

8. Pull your left foot back into a back stance with your left foot forward with a left knife hand high block.

8. 왼발 당겨 뒷굽이 왼 손날얼굴막기

9. Front kick with your right leg, landing forward into a back stance with your right foot forward with a right supported knife hand low block.

9. 오른발 앞차고 왼 뒷굽이 오른 아래손날거들어막기

10. Keeping your stance, slowly make an outward middle block for 8 seconds.

10. 발자세 그대로 오른 바깥막기(8초)

# Jitae
지태

11. Front kick with your left leg, landing forward into a back stance with your left foot forward with a left supported knife hand low block.

11. 왼발 앞차고 오른 뒷굽이 왼 아래손날거들어막기

12. Slightly step forward with your left foot into a left leg long stance with a slow left hand high block for 8 seconds.

12. 왼발 내디뎌 앞굽이 왼 얼굴막기 (8초)

13. Step forward into a right leg long stance and a forward diamond punch (right hand punch, left hand high block).

13. 오른발 내디뎌 앞굽이 오른 금강앞지르기

14. Keeping your stance, make an inward chest block with your left hand, followed by a supported right inward chest block.

14. 발자세 그대로 왼 안막고 오른 안막기(왼손은 거든다.)

# Jitae
## 지태

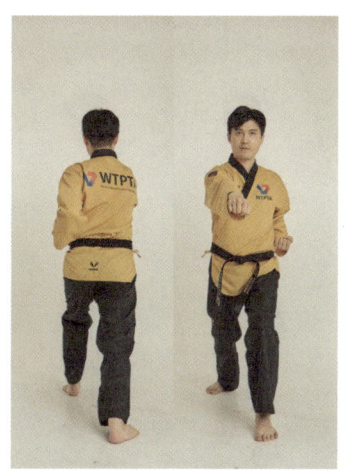

15. Step back into a back stance with your left foot forward with a left knife hand low block.

15. 오른발 물러디뎌
    뒷굽이 왼 손날아래막기

16. Front kick with your right leg, landing back into a left leg long stance with a double punch (right, then left hand punch in succession).

16. 오른발 앞차고 왼 앞굽이
    두번지르기(오른-왼)

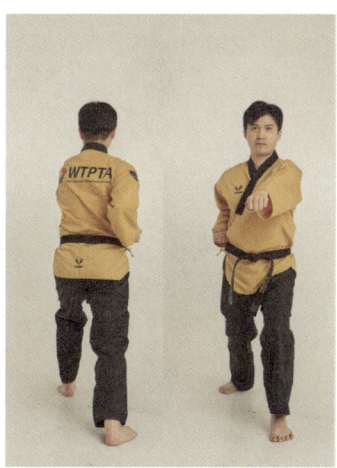

17. Turn to the left and step to the left with your left foot into a riding horse stance with a bull horn block.

17. 시선 왼쪽으로 이동하며
    왼발 물러디뎌 주춤서기 황소막기

18. Keeping your stance, look left toward the back and make a left hand low block.

18. 발자세 그대로 왼 아래막기

# Jitae
## 지태

19. Keeping your stance, look right toward the front and make a right outward single knife hand outwaed block.

19. 발자세 그대로 오른 손날옆막기

20. Keeping your stance, make a hammer fist side target strike (right hand target, left hand hammer fist) with Kihap.

20. 발자세 그대로
 왼 메주먹표적안치기(얼굴 높이, 기합)

21. Lift your right foot up into a crane stance with a right hand low block, followed by a left small hinge.

21. 왼 학다리서기 오른 아래옆막고 왼 작은돌쩌귀

22. Side kick with your right leg, landing in place with your feet together. Look toward the back and lift your left leg up into a crane stance with a left hand low block, followed by a right small hinge.

22. 오른발 옆차고 오른 학다리서기 왼 아래옆막고 오른 작은돌쩌귀

# Jitae
## 지태

23. Side kick with your left leg, landing forward into a left leg long stance with a right hand punch.

23. 왼발 옆차고 왼 앞굽이 오른 몸통지르기

24. Step forward into a right leg long stance with a right hand punch with Kihap.

24. 오른발 내디뎌 앞굽이 오른 몸통지르기(기합)

25. Turn 270° to the left and step forward into a back stance with your left foot forward with a left supported knife hand low block.

25. 왼쪽으로 돌아 오른 뒷굽이 왼 아래손날거들어막기

26. Step forward into a back stance with your right foot forward with a right supported knife hand middle block.

26. 오른발 내디뎌 뒷굽이 오른 손날거들어바깥막기

# Jitae
# 지태

27. Step back with your right foot and turn 180° to the right, making a back stance with your right foot forward and a right supported knife hand low block.

27. 오른쪽으로 돌아 왼 뒷굽이 오른 아래손날거들어막기

28. Step forward into a back stance with your left foot forward and a left supported knife hand middle block.

28. 왼발 내디뎌 뒷굽이 왼 손날거들어바깥막기

Baro
바로

Important movements: Geumgang Momtongjireugi (diamond forward punch), Momtong Anmakgi-Momtong Geodeureomakgi (inward chest block then supported inward chest block), Mejumeok Pyojeokchigi (hammer fist side target strike)
Important stances: Hakdariseogi (crane stance)

# Chonkwon
## 천권

Chonkwon represents the great power of heaven, which is the foundation of all things and the universe itself. The infinite power of heaven signifies creation, change, and perfection. People feared and revered great powers that they did not understand, such that the people named these powers the heavens.

In the distant past, more than 9,000 years ago, King Hwanin, the founder of the Korean people, was called the King of Heaven. He established a capital city in the sky near the heavenly sea and heavenly mountains, where the thought and practice of Taekwondo emerged from the Korean people, the nation of heaven. Chonkwon Poomsae was created according to the grandiose history of the origin of Taekwondo.

Techniques that are introduced in this poomsae are Nalgaepyeogi (wings spread), Bamjumeok Chijireugi (upper cut with walnut fists), Hwidulleomakgi (swing block), Jabadanggigi (pull), Pyeonson Oesanteul Arae-makge (open hand single mountain block), Geumgang Yeopjireugi (diamond side punch), Taesanmilgi (big mountion push), Jajeunbal (multiple sliding steps).

The essence of Chonkwon is displayed through its large movements and its gentle bending of arm motions. (Kukkiwon, 2022).

Shape of Poomsae: 'ㅜ' (The shape of the Poomsae depicts a person who has descended from heaven. The depicted person is one that lives according to the will of heaven, who receives strength from heaven, and who supports heaven.)

Number of Poom : 26

천권은 만물의 근본이며 우주 그 자체이기도 한 하늘이 가진 대능력을 의미한다. 우주 자연의 변화는 창조, 변화, 완성을 나타낸다.
새로운 동작은 날개펴기, 두 밤주먹 치지르기, 편손외산틀막기, 금강옆지르기, 태산밀기 등이고 보법으로 잦은발이 나오며 동작의 특징은 움직임이 큰 동작과 팔동작이 완만한 곡선을 이루어 천권 큰 사상을 담았다(국기원, 2022).
품새선: 'ㅜ'는 하늘에서 내리는 사람과 하늘의 뜻에 의한 사람 그리고 하늘로부터 힘을 받은 사람과 하늘을 받드는 사람인 하늘사람이란 뜻과 하늘과 사람이랑 뜻을 함께 지니고 있다.
품수:26품

# Chonkwon
# 천권

Kyopson Jinbiseogi

겹손 준비

1. From a closed stance, bring your hands up to your chest and slowly push both hands to the side, with your palms facing away from you for 5 seconds.

1. 모아서기 날개펴기

2. Make a large circular motion with both hands and step back with your left leg into a right leg tiger stance with a double chestnut fist upper-cut punch.

2. 두 팔로 원을 그리며 왼발 물러디뎌 오른 범서기 두 밤주먹 치지르기

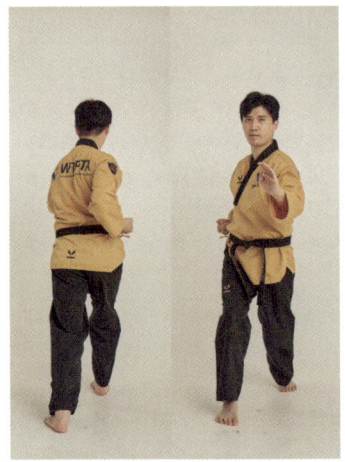

3. Step forward into a right leg long stance with a left twisted outward knife hand block.

3. 오른발 내디뎌 앞굽이 왼 손날비틀어바깥막기

4. Slowly rotate your left wrist until your palm faces upward and make a fist. Then, slowly pull back your left hand while stepping forward into a left leg long stance with a right hand punch for a total of 8 seconds.

4. 왼손 감아 잡아당기며 왼발 내디뎌 앞굽이 오른 몸통지르기(8초)

# Chonkwon
## 천권

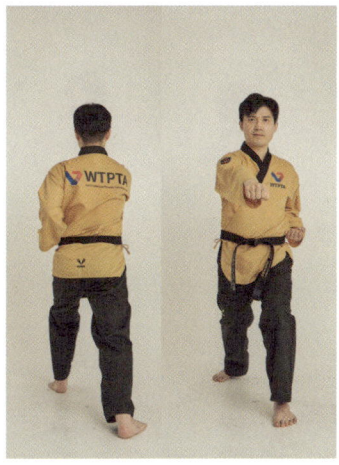

5. Keeping your stance, make a right twisted high block.

5. 발자세 그대로 오른 손날비틀어바깥막기

6. Slowly rotate your right wrist until your palm faces upward and make a fist. Then, slowly pull back your right hand while stepping forward into a right leg long stance with a left hand punch for a total of 8 seconds.

6. 오른손 감아 잡아당기며 오른발 내디뎌 앞굽이 왼 몸통지르기(8초)

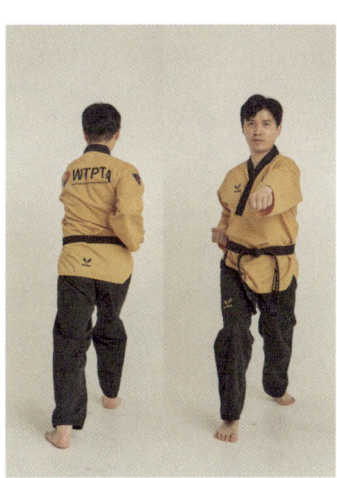

7. Keeping your stance, make a left twisted outward knife hand block.

7. 발자세 그대로 왼 손날비틀어바깥막기

8. Rotate your left wrist until your palm face upwards and make a fist. Pull back your fist and left leg side kick with Kihap, landing forward in a left leg long stance with a left hand low block.

8. 왼손 감아 잡아당기며 왼발 옆차고(기합) 왼 앞굽이 왼 아래막기

# Chonkwon
# 천권

9. Step forward into a right leg long stance with a right hand punch.

9. 오른발 내디뎌 앞굽이 오른 몸통지르기

10. Turn 270° to the left and step forward into a back stance with your left foot forward with supported outward inner wrist block.

10. 왼쪽으로 돌아 오른 뒷굽이 왼 안팔목거들어바깥막기

11. Keeping your stance, swing your left hand in a large circular motion into an outer block, then punch with your left hand.

11. 발자세 그대로 왼팔목 젖혀내며(아래에서 위로) 왼 지르기

# Chonkwon
## 천권

12. Make a circular left hand high block motion and step forward into a back stance with your right foot forward with a right hand punch.

12. 왼팔목 위로 젖혀내며 오른발 내디뎌 뒷굽이 오른 지르기

13. Step back with your right foot and turn 180° to the right, making a back stance with your right foot forward with a supported outward inner wrist block.

13. 오른쪽으로 돌아 왼 뒷굽이 오른 안팔목거들어바깥막기

14. Keeping your stance, swing your right hand in a large circular motion into an outer block, then punch with your right hand.

14. 발자세 그대로 오른팔목 젖혀내며(아래에서 위로) 오른 지르기

# Chonkwon
# 천권

15. Make a circular right hand high block motion and step forward into a back stance with your left foot forward with a left hand punch.

15. 오른팔목 위로 젖혀내며 왼발 내디뎌 뒷굽이 왼 지르기

16. Turn left toward the back and step forward into a left leg long stance with a right twisted outward inner wrist block.

16. 왼쪽으로 돌아 왼 앞굽이 오른 안팔목비틀어바깥막기

17. Keeping your stance, punch with your left hand.

17. 발자세 그대로 왼 몸통지르기

18. Front kick with your right leg, landing forward into a right leg long stance with a right hand punch.

18. 오른발 앞차고 오른 앞굽이 오른 몸통지르기

# Chonkwon
# 천권

19. Pull your right leg back into a back stance with your right leg forward with a right supported knife hand low block.

19. 오른발 당겨 왼 뒷굽이 오른 아래손날거들어막기

20. Make short sliding steps with your right then left foot, landing with your feet close together, while making a right outward inner wrist block and hitting your left hand target. Make short sliding steps with your right, then left foot into a back stance with your right foot forward with a right hand low block, hitting your left hand target. Clench your left fist to make a right hand supported low block.

20. 잦은발(오른발-왼발) 왼 뒷굽이 오른 안팔목바깥막고 오른 아래거들어막기

21. Slightly step forward with your right foot into a riding horse stance with a right diamond side punch (right hand punch, left hand high block).

21. 오른발 옮겨디뎌 주춤서기 금강옆지르기

22. Turn 360° to the left, jumping with a right leg crescent kick to your left hand target. Land forward in a riding horse stance with a right diamond side punch (right hand punch, left hand high block).

22. 왼쪽으로 뛰어 돌며 오른발 표적차고 주춤서기 금강옆지르기

# Chonkwon
# 천권

23. Turn left toward the front, making a back stance with your left foot forward and a slow motion open hand single mountain block for 5 seconds.

23. 왼쪽으로 돌아 오른 뒷굽이 편손외산틀막기(5초)

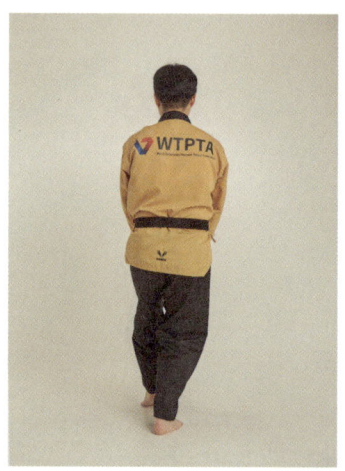
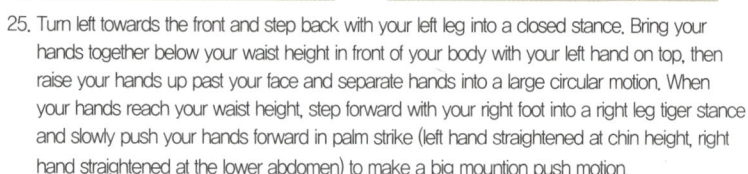

24. Turn right toward the back, making a back stance with your right foot forward and a slow motion open hand single mountain block for 5 seconds.

24. 오른쪽으로 돌아 왼 뒷굽이 편손외산틀막기(5초)

25. Turn left towards the front and step back with your left leg into a closed stance. Bring your hands together below your waist height in front of your body with your left hand on top, then raise your hands up past your face and separate hands into a large circular motion. When your hands reach your waist height, step forward with your right foot into a right leg tiger stance and slowly push your hands forward in palm strike (left hand straightened at chin height, right hand straightened at the lower abdomen) to make a big mountion push motion.

25. 왼쪽으로 돌아 모아서기(왼발 이동) 단전 앞 겹손에서 머리 위로 올려 원그리며 헤쳐막고 오른발 내디뎌 범서기 태산밀기(오른손 아래)

# Chonkwon
# 천권

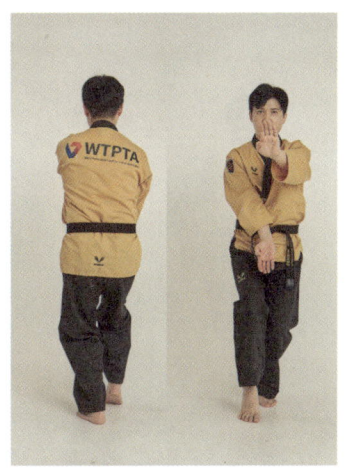
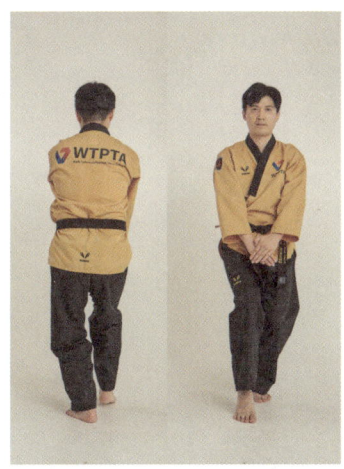

26. Step back with your right foot into a closed stance. Bring your hands together below your waist height in front of your body with your left hand on top, then raise your hands up past your face and separate hands into a large circular motion. When your hands reach your waist height, step forward with your left foot into a left leg tiger stance and slowly push your hands forwards in palm strike, (right hand straightened at chin height, left hand straightened at the lower abdomen) to make a big mountion push motion.

26. (오른발 당기며)모아서기 단전 앞 겹손에서 머리 위로 올려 원그리며 헤쳐막고 왼발 내디뎌 범서기 태산밀기(왼손 아래)

# Chonkwon
## 천권

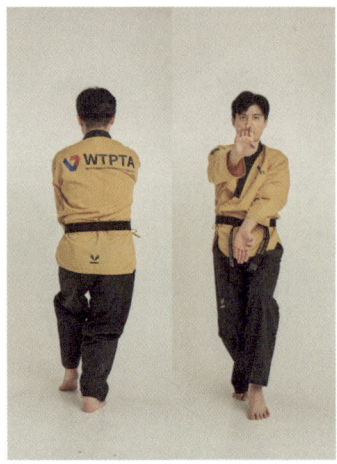
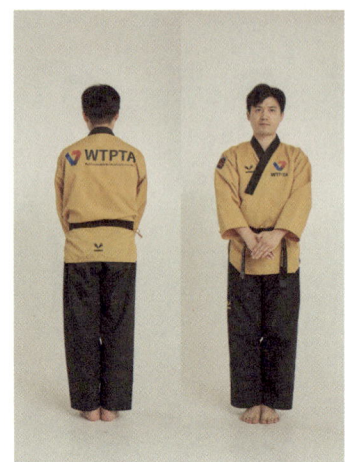

Baro
바로

Important movements: Sonnal Momtong Biteureomakgi (twisted outward knife hand block), Geumgang Yeopjireugi (diamond side punch), Taesanmilgi (big mountain push), Ttwieo Dora Pyojeokchagi (jumping tornado inward target crescent kick).
Important stance: Jajeunbal (multiple sliding steps).

# Hansu
# 한수

Hansu refers to water, which is the source of nurture for all forms of life. Hansu is symbolic of birth and growth of life, strength and weakness, great tolerance, cohesion, and adaptability. Han has many meanings, such as one, many, big, middle, equal, full, together, gather, wait, long, etc. Han may also refer to the root of everything, as well as heaven.
Techniques that are introduced in this Poomsae are Sonnaldeung Hecheomakgi (back of knife hand scatter block), Geodeureo Khaljaebi (supported arc hand strike), Anpalmok Arae Pyojeokmakgi (low inward inner wrist terget block), Sonnal Geumgangmakgi (kinfe hand diamond block), and Gyeotdariseogi (assist stance). The practice of this Poomsae should be performed with the softness of water, but continuously as water drops converge to form a sea. (Kukkiwon, 2022).
Shape of Poomsae: '水' (This Poomsae is in the shape of the chinese character for water.)
Number of Poom : 27

한수는 만물의 생명을 키워주는 근원이 되는 한물을 의미하며 한물은 생명의 탄생과 성장, 강함과 약함, 큰 포용력과 융화력 그리고 적응력을 나타낸다. 한은 "하나"라는 뜻과 많다, 크다, 가운데, 같다 가득하다, 함께, 모인다, 잠깐, 오래 등 여러 가지 많은 뜻을 가지고 있으며 하늘이라는 뜻과 모든 것의 뿌리라는 뜻도 담겨져있다.
이런 의미와 부술 수도 끊을 수도 없는 물의 특성을 기술에 적용하여 한수가 꾸며졌다.
새로운 동작은 손날등헤쳐막기, 두 메주먹 안치기, 아금손거들어앞치기, 아래안팔목표적안막기, 손날금강막기 등이며 서기는 곁다리가 있고 동작의 연습은 물처럼 유연하게 하되 한방울의 물이 큰바다를 이루는 것처럼 꾸준히 해야한다(국기원, 2022).
품새선 : '水'는 물과 민족의 핏줄인 한가람 그리고 커짐을 뜻한다.
품수 : 27품

# Hansu
# 한수

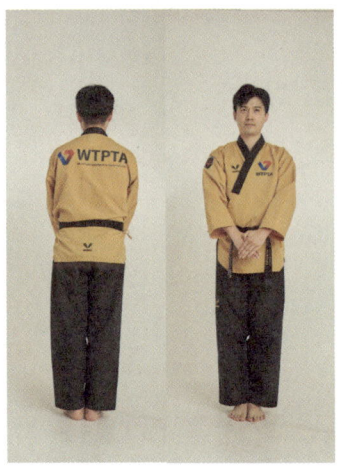

Kyopson Junbiseogi

겹손 준비

1. Step forward into a left leg long stance with a knife hand scatter block

1. 왼발 앞으로 내디뎌
   앞굽이 손날등헤쳐막기

2. Step forward into a right leg long stance with an inward double hammer fist strike to the ribcage.

2. 오른발 내디뎌 앞굽이
   두메주먹 안치기

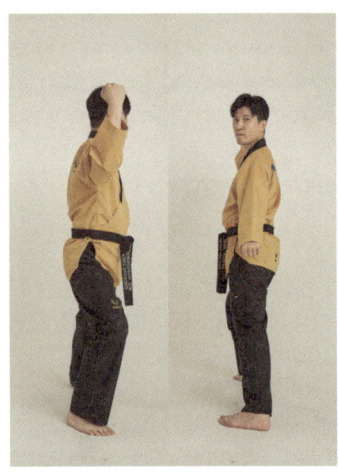

3. Step back with your right leg into a long right leg parallel stance with a single mountain block (right outward inner wrist high block, left hand low block).

3. 오른발 물러디뎌 앞굽이 외산틀막기
   (모앞굽이 형태로)

4. Slightly step forward with your left foot into a left leg long stance with a right hand punch.

4. 왼발 옮겨디뎌 왼 앞굽이
   오른 몸통지르기

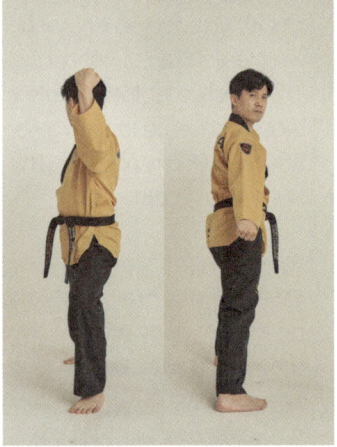

5. Step back with your left foot into a long left parallel stance with a single mountain block (left hand inward inner wrist high block, right hand low block).

5. 왼발 물러디뎌 왼 앞굽이 외산틀막기
   (모앞굽이 형태로)

# Hansu
# 한수

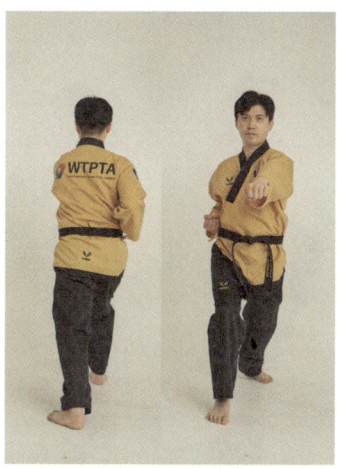

6. Slightly step forward with your right foot into a right leg long stance with a left hand punch.

6. 오른발 옮겨디뎌 오른 앞굽이 왼 몸통지르기

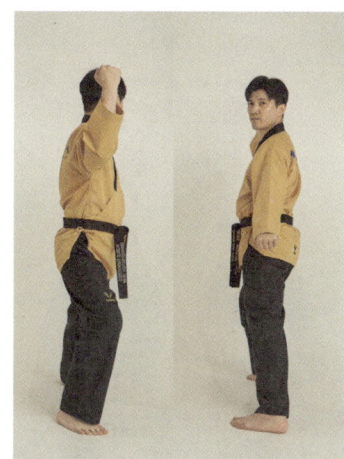

7. Step back with your right leg into a long right parallel stance with a single mountain block (right outward inner wrist high block, left hand low block).

7. 오른발 물러디뎌 오른 앞굽이 외산틀막기 (모앞굽이 형태로)

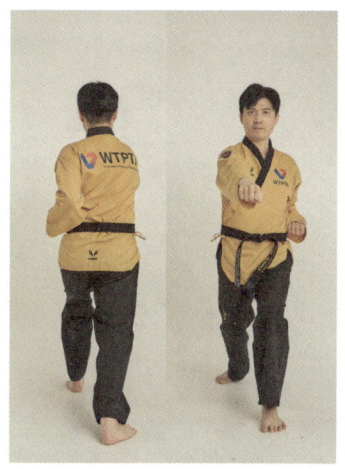

8. Slightly step forward with your left foot into a left leg long stance with a right hand punch.

8. 왼발 옮겨디뎌 왼 앞굽이 오른 몸통지르기

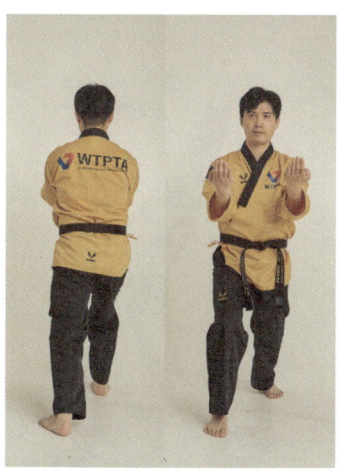

9. Step forward into a right leg long stance with a back of knife hand scatter block.

9. 오른발 내디뎌 앞굽이 손날등헤쳐막기

10. Turn 45° to the left and step forward into a left leg long stance and a supported left arc hand strike.

10. 왼발 정면 왼쪽 사선 방향으로 내디뎌 앞굽이 왼 아금손거들어앞치기

11. Step forward with your right leg into a cross stance with with flipped double fist punch.

11. 오른발 내디뎌 곁다리서기 두주먹젖혀지르기

# Hansu
## 한수

12. Step back with your left leg into a riding horse stance with right inward low inner wrist target block (right hand inner wrist block, left hand target).

12. (시선유지)왼발 물러디뎌 주춤서기 오른 아래 안팔목 표적 안막기

13. Step back with your right leg into a back stance with your left foot forward with a knife hand diamond block (left hand high block, right hand low block).

13. 오른발 물러디뎌 뒷굽이 손날금강막기

14. Turn 90° left toward the back left corner and lift your left foot up into a crane stance with a right small hinge block.

14. 시선 후면 왼쪽 사선 방향으로 이동하며 오른 학다리서기 오른 작은돌쩌귀

15. Side kick with your left leg, landing forward into a left leg long stance with a swallow-shaped strike (left knife hand high block, right knife hand neck strike).

15. 왼발 옆차고 왼 앞굽이 오른 제비품안치기(목 높이)

16. Front kick with your right leg, landing the distance of one long stance forward with a stomp into a cross stance with a right back fist forward face strike with Kihap.

16. 오른발 앞차고 짓찧으며 뒤꼬아서기 오른 등주먹앞치기(얼굴높이, 기합)

# Hansu
# 한수

17. Turn left toward the front right corner and step forward with your left foot into a riding horse stance with a left knife hand side strike to the neck.

17. 왼쪽으로 돌아(왼발 이동) 주춤서기 왼 손날옆치기

18. Crescent kick with your right leg to your left hand target, landing forward in riding horse stance with a right elbow target strike.

18. 오른발 표적안차고 주춤서기 오른 팔꿈치표적앞치기

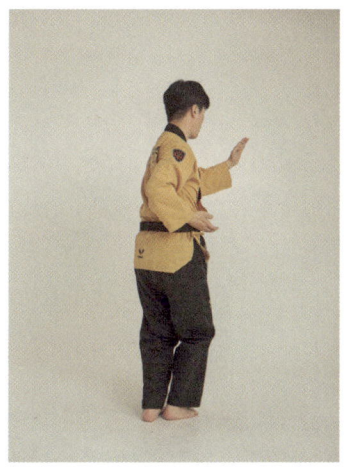

19. Step forward with your left foot into a closed stance, then step forward with your right foot into a right leg long stance with a supported right arc hand strike.

19. 모아서기 후(왼발 이동) 오른발 내디뎌 앞굽이 오른 아금손거들어앞치기

# Hansu
## 한수

20. Step forward with your left leg into a cross stance with flipped double fist punch.

20. 왼발 내디뎌 곁다리서기 두주먹 젖혀지르기

21. Step back with your right leg into a riding horse stance with a left inward low inner wrist target block (left hand inner wrist block, right hand target).

21. (시선유지)오른발 물러디뎌 주춤서기 왼 아래 안팔목 표적 안막기

22. Step back with your left leg into a back stance with your right foot forward with a knife hand diamond block (right hand high block, left hand low block).

22. 왼발 물러디뎌 뒷굽이 손날금강막기

23. Turn 90° right toward the back right corner, lifting your right leg up into a crane stance with a left small hinge block

23. 시선 후면 오른쪽 사선 방향으로 이동하며 왼 학다리서기 왼 작은돌쩌귀

24. Side kick with your right leg, landing forward in a right leg long stance with a swallow-shaped strike (right knife hand high block, left knife hand neck strike).

24. 오른발 옆차고 오른 앞굽이 왼 제비품안치기(목 높이)

# Hansu
## 한수

25. Front kick with your left leg, landing the distance of one long stance forward with a stomp into a cross stance with a left back fist forward face strike with Kihap.

25. 왼발 앞차고 짓찧으며 뒤꼬아서기 왼 등주먹앞치기(얼굴 높이, 기합)

26. Turn right toward the front left corner and step forward with your right foot into a riding horse stance with a right knife hand side strike to the neck.

26. 오른쪽으로 돌아(오른발 이동) 주춤서기 오른 손날옆치기

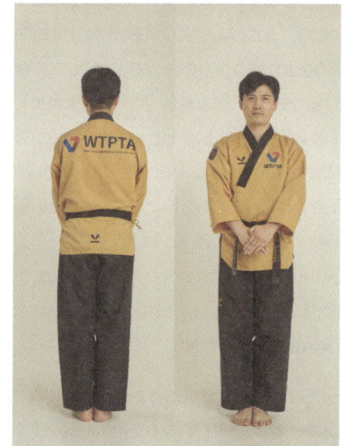

27. Crescent kick with your left leg into your right hand target, landing forward in a riding horse stance with a left elbow target strike.

27. 왼발 표적안차고 주춤서기 왼 팔꿈치표적앞치기

Baro
바로

Important movements: Mejumeok Yangyeopguri Anchigi (Hammer fist both waist strike), Geodeureo Khaljaebi (supported arc hand strike), Anpalmok Arae Pyojeokmakgi (low inward inner wrist target block)
Important stance: Gyeotdariseogi (assist stance)

# Ilyeo
일여

Ilyeo means the ideology of the great monk of Silla, Wonhyo. The Wonhyo ideology refers to the high heavenly belief that the mind (spirit) and the body (material) are one. While performing Poomsae, one learns that all techniques and movements are shaped and executed differently. Ultimately, Poomsae is based on the deep truth of martial arts in which the spirit and movement are united.

Techniques that are introduced in this Poomsae are Oesanteul Yeopchagi (single mountion block with side kick), Dusonpyeo Biteureo Jabadanggigi (open hand twist pulling), Ttwieo Yeopchagi (jumping side kick), and Ogeumseogi (reverse crance stance).

The ready stance is The Bojumeok Moaseogi (covered fist ready stance). Since it is the last Poomsae of Taekwondo, the Bojumeok Moaseogi (covered fist ready stance) carries the meaning of unification of all the Poomsaes together in Taekwondo. In Bojumeok Moaseogi (covered fist ready stance), energy flows through the body as the two hands are joined together and wrapped, signifying alignment of energy through Taekwondo(Kukkiwon, 2022).

Shape of Poomsae: '卍' (It was used as a symbol of Buddhism to commemorate the Buddhist priest Wonhyo, and it means a perfect self-effacement state in which one's essence, body, and actions are in harmony.)
Number of Poom : 23

Ready stance (covered fist): With your feet together in a closed stance, grasp your right fist with your left open hand to make a covered fist. Inhale, and slowly raise your hands from the lower part of the abdomen to the solar plexus. Exhale, and raise your hands to the height of your philtrum.

일여는 원효대사의 일여사상을 가리킨다. 마음(정신)과 몸(물질)은 하나이며, 점과 선이 결국에는 원과 같은 하나가 되는 것으로 본다. 태권도의 다양한 기법과 동작들도 마찬가지로 궁극적으로 합쳐지고 나아가 정신과 동작이 일체가 되는 깊은 무예로서 태권도 수련이 완성된다는 진리를 지닌 품새이다(국기원, 2022).
품새선:' 卍' 원효대사의 일여사상을 나타낸다.
품수: 23

# Ilyeo
## 일여

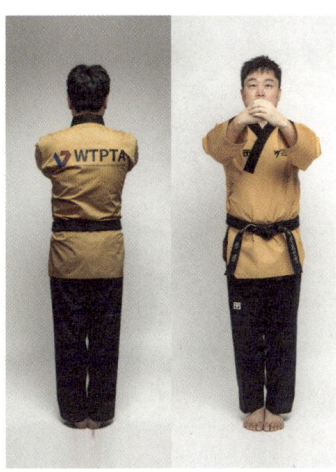

Bojumeok Junbiseogi

보주먹 준비

1. Step forward into a back stance with your left foot forward with left supported knife hand middle block.

1. 왼발을 앞으로 내디뎌 뒷굽이 왼 손날거들어바깥막기

2. Step forward into a right leg long stance with a right hand punch.

2. 오른발 내디뎌 앞굽이 오른 몸통지르기

3. Turn toward the left and step into a back stance with your left foot forward with a slow diamond block for 8 seconds (left hand low block, right hand high block).

3. 왼발 왼쪽으로 내디뎌 오른 뒷굽이 금강막기(시선 왼쪽, 8초)

4. Turn left toward the back and step into a back stance with your left leg forward with a left supported knife hand middle block, followed by a right hand punch.

4. 왼발 왼쪽으로 내디뎌 뒷굽이 왼 손날거들어바깥막고 오른 몸통지르기

# Ilyeo
# 일여

 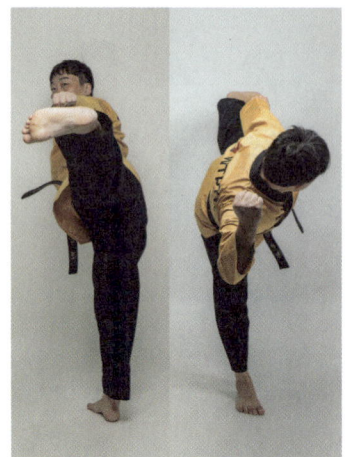

5. Step forward with a hop, landing with your right foot into a right reversed crane stance (left foot hooked onto the back of your right knee) with a left supported upright thrust with Kihap.

5. 오른발 앞으로 뛰어 내디뎌
   오른 오금서기 왼 거들어세워찌르기(기합)

6. Side kick with your left foot, simultaneously performing a single mountain block (right outward inner wrist high block, left hand low block) with your kick, landing forward in a back stance with your left foot forward and a face crossing block (right hand on top).

6. 외산틀 옆차기(외산틀과 왼 옆차기 동시)
   오른 뒷굽이 얼굴엇걸어막기

7. Open your hands and twist your hands in a circular motion around your wrists while stepping forward into a right leg long stance with a right hand punch.

7. 엇걸어 손 비틀어 잡아당기며 오른발
   내디뎌 앞굽이 오른 몸통지르기

8. Turn to the left and step into a back stance with your left foot forward with a slow diamond block for 8 seconds (left hand low block, right hand high block).

8. 왼발 왼쪽으로 내디뎌
   뒷굽이 금강막기(시선 왼쪽, 8초)

9-1. Turn left toward the front and step into a back stance with your left leg forward with a left supported knife hand middle block.

9-1. 왼발 왼쪽으로 내디뎌 뒷굽이
   왼 손날거들어바깥막기

# Ilyeo
# 일여

9-2. Keep the stance the same, punch with your right hand.

9-2. 발자세 그대로 오른 몸통지르기

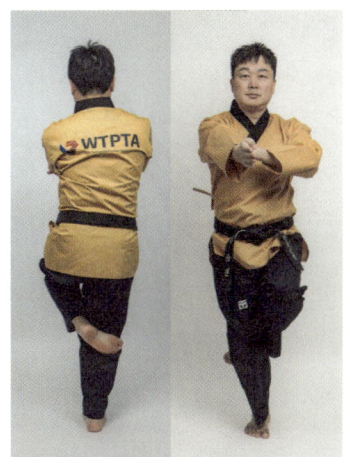

10. Step forward with a hop, landing with your right foot into a right reversed crane stance (left foot hooked onto the back of your right knee) with a right supported upright thrust with Kihap.

10. 오른발 앞으로 뛰어 내디뎌 오른 오금세기 오른 거들어세워찌르기(기합)

11. Left leg side kick to the left while simultaneously performing a single mountain block (right outward inner wrist high block, left hand low block) with your kick, landing forward in a back stance with your left foot forward with a face crossing block (right hand on top).

11. 왼쪽으로 외산틀 옆차고(외산틀과 왼 옆차기 동시) 오른 뒷굽이 얼굴엇걸어막기

12. Open your hands and twist your hands in a circular motion around your wrists while stepping forward into a right leg long stance with a right hand punch.

12. 엇걸은 손 비틀어 잡아당기며 오른발 내디뎌 앞굽이 오른 몸통지르기

13. Turn left toward the back and step into a back stance with your left foot forward with a slow diamond block for 8 seconds (left hand low block, right hand high block).

13. 왼발 왼쪽으로 내디뎌 뒷굽이 금강막기(시선 왼쪽, 8초)

# Ilyeo
# 일여

14. Turn to the left and step with your left foot into a closed stance with your feet together and slowly pull your fists to your hips for 5 seconds.

14. 왼쪽으로 돌아 모아서기 두 주먹 허리(왼발 당겨, 5초)

15. Front kick with your right leg, landing forward and jumping into left leg jumping side kick. Land into a back stance with your left foot forward with a face crossing block (left hand on top).

15. 오른발 앞차고 왼발 뛰어옆차고 오른뒷굽이 얼굴엇걸어막기

16. Open your hands and twist your hands in a circular motion around your wrists while stepping forward into a right leg long stance with a right hand punch.

16. 엇걸은 손 비틀어 잡아당기며 오른발 내디뎌 앞굽이 오른 몸통지르기

17. Turn left toward the front and step forward into a back stance with your left foot forward with a slow diamond block for 8 seconds (left hand low block, right hand high block).

17. 왼발 왼쪽으로 내디뎌 뒷굽이 금강막기(시선 왼쪽, 8초)

# Ilyeo
# 일여

18. Turn to the left and step with your left foot into a closed stance with your feet together and slowly pull your fists to your hips for 5 seconds.

18. 왼쪽으로 돌아 모아서기 두 주먹 허리(왼발 당겨, 5초)

19. Front kick with your left leg, landing forward and jumping into right leg jumping side kick. Land into a back stance with your right foot forward with a face crossing block (left hand on top).

19. 왼발 앞차고 오른발 뛰어옆차고 왼 뒷굽이 얼굴엇걸어막기

 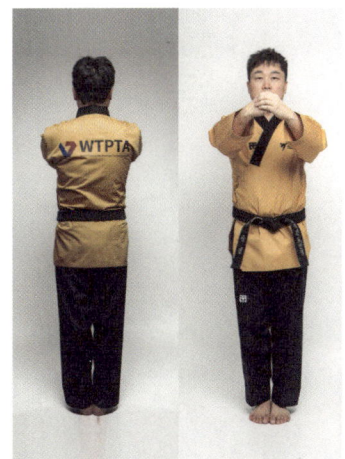

Baro
바로

Critical Motions: Ttwieo Yeopchagi (jumping side kick), Oesanteul Yeopchagi (single mountion block with side kick), Otgoreo Eolgulmakgi (face crossing block).
Critical Stance: Ogeumseogi (reversed crane stance).